Inside the World of Computing

Inside the World of Computing

Technologies, Uses, Challenges

Jean-Loïc Delhaye

WILEY

First published 2021 in Great Britain and the United States by ISTE Ltd and John Wiley & Sons, Inc.

ISTE Ltd
27-37 St George's Road
London SW19 4EU
UK

www.iste.co.uk

John Wiley & Sons, Inc.
111 River Street
Hoboken, NJ 07030
USA

www.wiley.com

Library of Congress Control Number: 2020951001

British Library Cataloguing-in-Publication Data
A CIP record for this book is available from the British Library
ISBN 978-1-78630-665-4

Contents

Foreword

Here is a book for those among us who are at the dawn of the 21st century. It invites us on a journey to the heart of this new digital world, whose "shores" were discovered a little more than half a century ago. This new world is revolutionizing our present lives and is going to have an even greater impact on future generations.

Computer science is a young science that has progressed exponentially but already has its history. This book does not pretend to have an exhaustive body of knowledge about computer science; there are a plethora of excellent books on this topic! Rather, it conveys a personal vision of this vast field through a professional life that is in constant "synergy" with research and innovation in computer science. As a privileged witness of this period, Jean-Loïc Delhaye invites us to journey through the progress that marked this "revolutionary" era.

In contrast to other sciences, such as mathematics, computer science (digital science) was created in close connection with computer technology. This is what contributes to its originality, and also its difficulty, as the development of technology is so fast. With the benefit of hindsight, Jean-Loïc Delhaye introduces us to the essential components of a digital environment, from computers to networks, from operating systems to the most advanced and popular applications.

The first chapter focuses on the basic "component", the computer. It takes us back in time, from Pascal's arithmetic machine, to the well-known calculator, to classic electronic computers (von Neumann architecture), and then up to supercomputers (which were the domain of Jean-Loïc Delhaye's predilection for several years). This chapter is a remarkable concentration of several decades of progress leading up to the processors and computers that now surround us in our daily lives.

One of the key developments in recent years has been the emergence of computer networks. Indeed, what could be more natural than to allow different computers to communicate with each other and cooperate in order to carry out increasingly complex tasks? Chapter 2 gives us a complete overview of the characteristics of the various networks and inevitably leads to discussions on one of the great inventions of the end of the 20th century: the Internet. In just a few pages, Jean-Loïc Delhaye succeeds in allowing us to discover this mysterious world of computer networks, a world that he came into close contact with during his career.

These first two chapters provide the hardware basis on which it is possible to "develop" systems and all kinds of applications. In order to solve a problem, it is necessary, starting from a precise description of the problem, to design a proper solution. This solution, called an algorithm, takes the form of a "sequence" of commands that "transform" data into a "result". This sequence of commands is, *a priori*, independent of any machine. For an execution on a given machine, in a given environment, this algorithm will be translated into software (or program) that is expressed in a computer language. Chapter 3 is entirely devoted to software and constitutes an excellent overview, even going as far as questioning legal protection (a subject on which Jean-Loïc Delhaye acquired a rare skill during his years at INRIA).

Chapter 4 deals with another crucial topic in computer science, namely that of data, its representation and storage. Unlike algorithms, which have been (and still are) a subject of both theoretical and practical study, data has often been neglected. The most common structures were tables, files, records and classical values such as integers, reals and Booleans. Then it was realized that data, although characterized by its values, was also especially characterized by the operations that could be applied to it, hence the numerous studies on data abstraction that gave rise to concepts such as classes and objects, common nowadays in programming languages. In this chapter, Jean-Loïc Delhaye gives a complete overview of data, including databases and "Big Data". Big Data is at the root of a major development in current computer science: by exploiting it "intelligently" and highlighting certain global properties used for various purposes; this subject will be discussed in Chapter 7.

Several subjects are at the heart of the concerns of research and development organizations today; it is a question of creating environments that will enable the development of tomorrow's applications. Jean-Loïc Delhaye has highlighted four essential "technologies" that concentrate much work around the world: 1) embedded systems, 2) artificial intelligence, 3) the Internet of tomorrow, 4) images and vision. For each of them, he proposes an overview of the issues and provides a panorama of the most current questions.

As the key technologies are developed, they constitute the "building blocks" from which large-scale applications can be implemented. In Chapter 6, Jean-Loïc Delhaye takes us on a rapid journey to the heart of tomorrow's world: robotics, virtual reality, health, mobility, energy, the factory of the future, etc. It is not only fascinating, but also speculative.

Chapter 7 addresses the difficult question of the societal impact of these advances. The major questions concern security when using these technologies, respect for privacy, the potential influence that these new systems (known as artificial intelligence systems) can have on citizens' freedom, and even the questioning of democracy as we know it. It also addresses the central issue, often forgotten by our elites and technologists, of the digital divide. We have to only look around us or travel a little to realize the extent of the problem. Jean-Loïc Delhaye approaches these subjects in a simple and factual way to provoke the reader's food for thought, and simply ends with the question: "What kind of world do we want?" That is the question!

To conclude, who should read this book, which covers the experience of an entire professional life? Readers of all ages who wish to better understand the history and advances of this science and technology that constitutes computer science (we are now talking about digital technology). There is no need for advanced knowledge to immerse oneself in reading (no equations, no complex diagrams, etc.), just common sense and curiosity! I would also recommend it to students in disciplines other than computer science; they will discover an interesting synthesis and perceive reality through the experiences of a real computer scientist. I believe that computer science students would also benefit from reading this book, which will give them, especially in the last chapters, an idea of the great challenges in computer science and may help them in their future professional choices!

Jean-Pierre BANÂTRE
Computer Scientist
Honorary Professor at the University of Rennes 1

Preface

I discovered computer science at the culmination of a university course in mathematics, with an MPhil, then a PhD in 1970 in theoretical computer science. I was fascinated by the potential of this science, which was then entering higher education, and the technologies that could already be seen, and I chose to dedicate my professional life to it. This is what I have done, working with researchers, engineers, and users in various settings: universities and research centers, companies (computer manufacturers, network operators, large and small companies and government agencies) and large computer centers at the service of research, supporting the transformations associated with these new technologies.

What an adventure!

Computer science was, in its early days, a field that concerned only a small number of specialists, the "computer scientists", also called computer engineers, according to the main orientation of their activity. It developed slowly, then more and more rapidly with regard to the "digital world", in which a large part of our planet lives today. It seems important to me to understand this new world, its technological bases, the motives of its main players, the impact on individuals and on society as a whole. This is the main objective of this book, which seeks to address the entirety of this phenomenon without going into the details of scientific or technical aspects, because many books dedicated to these aspects already exist.

The French term *"informatique"* (computer science) was coined in 1962 by Philippe Dreyfus, who was the director of Bull's *Centre national de calcul électronique*, or Bull's National Center for Electronic Computing, in the 1950s and a pioneer of the discipline in France. It is thought to be derived from the contraction of the words *"information"* and *"automatique"* (automatic).

In 1966, computer science was defined by the *Académie Française* (French council for matters pertaining to the French language) as the "science of rational processing, particularly by automatic machines, of information considered as the medium of human knowledge and communications in the technical, economic and social fields."

According to Gérard Berry, professor at the Collège de France, "the word 'computer science' refers to the science and technology of information processing and, by extension, the industry directly dedicated to these subjects."

What we call "computer science" is changing the way we work, invading our homes, becoming part of everyday objects and offering us new leisure activities. It is even at the origin of new modes of sociability, new professions and a new economy: it is everywhere!

Your smartphone is much more than just a phone: a high-quality digital camera, access to databases, integrated GPS, all kinds of applications, etc. You communicate very easily with your loved ones (and those less close to you!), for example, through social networks. The good (or bad) functioning of certain equipment in your home is directly related to small hardware and software: TV, appliances, remote control, security, etc. Many devices in modern cars are linked to computer science: combustion, ABS, cruise control, driving assistance, GPS, in-car TV, etc. The complete and detailed design of aircrafts is now based on modeling and simulation, right up to wind tunnel tests, which are carried out in "digital wind tunnels".

This is true in many other industrial sectors. Artistic creations increasingly use computers: cinema, photography, music, painting, etc. We even talk about "digital art" and artists creating a work of art from their own software, sometimes called an algorist. All fields of science are rapidly evolving thanks to the possibilities offered by computer science: medicine, meteorology and climatology, astronomy, biology, physics, chemistry, geology, mathematics, social sciences, economics, architecture, etc.

This "digitization" sometimes presents problems (malfunctions, bugs) and even risks (data theft, phishing, attacks from hackers, etc.). Not to mention the destruction of jobs, which will probably not be compensated by the creation of new ones.

The pillars of computer science can be represented as in Figure P.1.

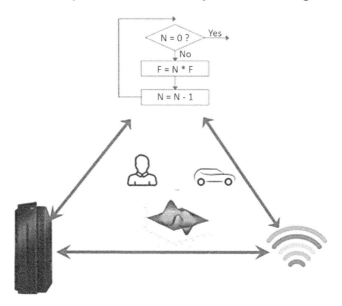

Figure P.1. *Pillars of computer science. For a color version of this figure, see www.iste.co.uk/delhaye/computing.zip*

These three pillars are:

– **hardware**: a set of equipment that ensures the processing of information. Hardware, especially processors, have evolved considerably since the first "computer";

– **communication means**: they enable the building of networks on various infrastructures (wires, radio waves, etc.);

– **software**: without it, nothing would work. Software contains sequences of instructions that describe in detail what the computer is being asked to do. These range from operating systems to application programs and user interfaces.

In the middle of these three pillars, which are at the heart of many scientific and technical fields, we find everything that we more or less use consciously in our daily lives and which is closely dependent on computer science.

This book briefly retraces the history of these three pillars, describes the main technologies associated with them and discusses the impact of computer science today through a few application areas, not forgetting the societal impact. It is divided into seven chapters.

Chapter 1 discusses some important concepts before retracing the history of hardware, from the first attempts at the automation of calculations, to today's computers with their diversity and architectures. It ends with questions about the future, both in terms of technology and environmental issues.

Communication networks play an essential role in the use of computers. **Chapter 2** presents their infrastructures and protocols, with a special focus on the Internet, and some applications with a focus on the Web. I also address an important aspect: the vulnerability of networks and the need to protect them against malicious attacks.

Chapter 3 is devoted to software, the translation of an algorithm and programming languages, with two levels of operating systems and applications. The main methods of development and validation of software are discussed, as well as the modes of distribution associated with "licenses".

Computers process data, and networks transport it. Representation and organization of the different types of data, from isolated "basic data", to files, to databases and Big Data that allow the creation of knowledge and even intelligence: this will be the subject of **Chapter 4**.

I have chosen four "technological bases" that enable us to build the services we have today and that are profoundly changing our daily lives: embedded systems in billions of devices, artificial intelligence, which is too often a selling point, the Internet, which enables people and computers themselves to communicate without spatial limits, and finally image processing and vision. These are the main aspects of **Chapter 5**.

There are countless areas of use for computing and networks, but I have chosen seven for **Chapter 6**: the robots we can see in factories (and now in houses), virtual reality and augmented reality that allow us to immerse ourselves and interact in virtual worlds, computing at the service of medical personnel and our health, the connected car that may soon be autonomous, the smart city, smart mobility, and finally the factory of the future, or factory 4.0.

Chapter 7 takes a step back from information and communication technologies to address some of the questions that their massive presence in all sectors of our lives seem to pose to society: various threats and the fight against cybercrime, the protection of personal data and privacy, the influence of these technologies on society, the dangers for democracy with the rise of large companies known as GAFA, the digital divide (because a large part of the planet is excluded from this digital world), the risks of a deviation in artificial intelligence, the creation of a class of "bionic humans" equipped with prostheses and, finally, the still-nascent doctrine of the immortal human and transhumanism.

To conclude, the question we must ask ourselves is: "what kind of society do we want?" Taking into account the "revolutions" that our societies have undergone, such as writing, printing and industry, none have had such a great impact on our lives and on society in general. We can be passionate about these "new technologies" – and I have been, since they have been at the center of my professional life – but we must keep control of their development and especially of their uses to avoid, if it is still possible, their use by groups seeking to dominate the world.

I wish you a good journey through this fascinating world.

Acknowledgments

This book has benefited greatly from the many exchanges I have had with Jean-Pierre Banâtre, a specialist recognized for his work on programming languages, parallel programming, software architectures and distributed systems. I had the chance to collaborate with him for more than 20 years, particularly in the management of research and development projects involving companies and public organizations.

Jean-Pierre Banâtre has given me friendly encouragement in this project, and I would like to express my gratitude to him here for his remarks, advice, encouragement and constructive criticism.

From the Calculator to the Supercomputer

1.1. Introduction

As noted in the Preface of this book, almost everyone uses computers, often unknowingly, in both professional and personal activities. The first computers weighed tons and took up a lot of space, while consuming a lot of energy. Today, our mobile phones have several tiny, energy-efficient computers built into them.

The history of these machines, known to us as computers, is marked by a few major steps that we present in this chapter. Let us first look at the evolution of hardware; we will deal with computer networks and software in the chapters that follow.

1.2. Some important concepts

Before describing the main steps that precede the construction of the first computers, let us clarify a few concepts that are important in this history.

1.2.1. *Information and data*

The word "information" covers a wide variety of fields. For example, our five senses (sight, smell, taste, hearing and touch) transmit information to our brains that is essential to our lives and even our survival.

Native Americans exchanged more structured information (e.g. as a way of inviting people to a tribal gathering) by means of smoke signals. These signals were coded and communicated, but they could not be stored.

Today, the word "information" is predominantly used to refer to events such as those presented in journalism (written or digital press, television news, radio, etc.). For our purposes, we will use a narrower definition: information is an element of knowledge that can be translated into a set of signals, according to a determined code, in order to be stored, processed or communicated.

Analog information is supported by a continuous signal, an oscillation in a power line, for example, or a bird song. Digital information is information that is symbolically coded with numbers (e.g. 384,400 for the distance in kilometers from the Earth to the Moon).

The theoretical concept of information was introduced from theoretical research on electrical communication systems. In a general sense, an information theory is a theory that aims to quantify and qualify the notion of information content present in a dataset. In 1948, the American mathematician Claude Shannon published the article, "A Mathematical Theory of Communication"[1] and has since been considered the father of information theory.

Data are what computers deal with, and we will come back to data in Chapter 4. These are raw quantities (numbers, texts, etc.) that will be digitized (converted into a series of numbers) so that they can be understood and manipulated by computers. Alphabetic characters (and other characters) can be easily digitized. A sound can be represented by a sequence of regularly sampled sound intensities, each digitally encoded. The information contained in digital data, that is, a number, depending on its context (on a pay slip, name and gross salary is information obtained from digital data based on their place on the pay slip).

---

1 Claude Shannon (1916–2001), an American engineer and mathematician, split his career between the Massachusetts Institute of Technology (MIT) and Bell Laboratories. In this article, he proposes a unit of information that is exactly the amount of information that a message can bring, which can only take two possible values, and with the same probability (e.g. 0 or 1).

1.2.2. *Binary system*

Computers process digital data encoded in base-2, and we will see why; but first, a brief description of this binary system.

We usually count in base-10, the decimal system that uses 10 digits (0, 1, 2, 3, 4, 5, 6, 7, 8, 9). To go beyond 9, we have to "change rank": if the rank of the units is full, we start the rank of the tens and reset the units to zero and so on. So, after 9, we have 10. When you get to 19, the row of units is full. So, we add a dozen and reset the unit rank to zero: we get to 20.

The binary system, or base-2 numbering system, uses only two symbols, typically "0" and "1". The number zero is written as "0", one is written as "1", two is written as "10", three is written as "11", four is written as "100", etc. In the binary system, the unit of information is called the bit (contraction of "binary digit"). For example, the base-2 number "10011" uses 5 bits.

It is quite easy to convert a decimal number (dn) to a binary number (bn). The simple solution is to divide the dn by 2; note the remainder of the division (0 or 1) which will be the last bit of the bn, start again with the previous quotient until the quotient is zero. For example, if the dn is 41, the division by 2 gives 20 + 1; the last bit (called rank 1) of the bn is 1; we divide 20 by 2, which gives 10 + 0; the bit of rank 2 is 0; we divide 10 by 2, which gives 5 + 0; the bit of rank 3 is 0; we divide 5 by 2, which gives 2 + 1; the bit of rank 4 is 1; we divide 2 by 2, which gives 1 + 0; the bit of rank 5 is 0; we divide 1 by 2, which gives 0 + 1; the bit of rank 6 is 1. So, the binary number is 101001.

The importance of the binary system for mathematics and logic was first understood by the German mathematician and philosopher Leibnitz in the 17th century. The binary system is at the heart of modern computing and electronics (calculators, computers, etc.) because the two numbers 0 and 1 are easily translated into the voltage or current flow.

1.2.3. *Coding*

In real life, the same information can be represented in different ways. For example, administrations use different forms to represent a date of birth: January 10, 1989; 01/10/1989; 10/JAN/89; etc. It is therefore necessary to agree on the same way of representing numbers and characters. This is coding.

Coding of information has existed for several years. For example, Morse code, named after its inventor Samuel Morse (1791–1872), is a telegraphic code using a conventional alphabet to transmit a text, using a series of long and short pulses.

1. A hyphen is equal to three dots.
2. Spacing between two elements of the same letter is equal to one dot.
3. Spacing between two letters is equal to three dots.
4. Spacing between two words is equal to seven dots.

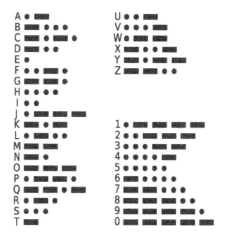

Figure 1.1. *Morse code*

Information coding refers to the means of formalizing information so that it can be manipulated, stored or transmitted. It is not concerned with the content but only with the form and size of the information to be coded.

With the advent of the computer, it has been necessary to develop data coding standards to facilitate their manipulation by computer tools around the world. We can represent the set of characters by binary codes of determined length. Binary is used for obvious reasons, one bit being the minimum amount of information that can be transmitted.

In computer science, we mainly use the **bit**, the **byte** (unit of information composed of 8 bits, which allows us to store a character such as a number or a letter) and the **word** (unit of information composed of 16 bits). We commonly use multiples: kilobyte (KB) for a thousand bytes, megabyte (MB) for a million bytes, gigabyte (GB) for a billion bytes and so on.

1.2.4. Algorithm

What should the computer do with this data encoded in binary numbers? What processing must it do? Adding two numbers is a trivial process, but we expect much more from a computer, and we must tell it what is expected of it!

The word algorithm comes from the name of the great Persian mathematician Al Khwarizmi (ca. 820 CE), who introduced decimal numeration (brought from India) in the West and taught the elementary rules of calculation related to it. The notion of the algorithm is thus historically linked to numerical manipulations, but it has gradually developed to deal with increasingly complex objects, texts, images, logical formulas, etc.

An algorithm, very simply, is a method, a systematic way of doing something: sorting objects, indicating a path to a lost tourist, multiplying two numbers or looking up a word in the dictionary. A recipe can be considered an algorithm if we can reduce its specificity to its constituent elements:

– input information (ingredients, materials used);

– simple elementary instructions (slicing, salting, frying, etc.), which are carried out in a precise order to achieve the desired result;

– a result: the prepared dish.

Algorithms, in the computer sense, appeared with the invention of the first machines equipped with automations. More precisely, in computer science, an algorithm is a finite and unambiguous sequence of operations or instructions to solve a problem or to obtain a result. It can be translated, thanks to a programming language, into a program executable by a computer.

Here is a simple example, the algorithm for determining the greatest common divisor (GCD) of two integers, a and b (Euclid's algorithm):

```
READ a and b
If b>a, then PERMUTE a and b
RETURN
r=the remainder of the division of a by b
If r is different from 0
 REPLACE a by b then b by r
 GO TO RETURN
WRITE b
END
```

Algorithms, in the real lives of computer scientists, are of course more complex. We have therefore tried to represent them in a more readable way and, above all, without any ambiguity, always possible in the interpretation of a text. Programming flowcharts are a standardized graphical representation of the sequence of operations and decisions carried out by a computer program. Figure 1.2 shows a flowchart of the Euclidean algorithm.

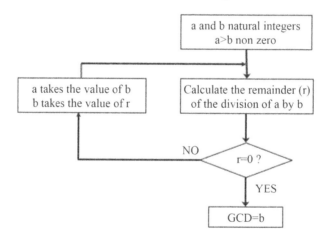

Figure 1.2. *Flowchart of the Euclidean algorithm*

We can usually solve a problem in several ways, and thus can write different algorithms, but all should lead to the same result. The algorithm's quality will be measured by criteria such as efficiency (speed of obtaining the result), the quantity of resources consumed, the accuracy of the result obtained, etc.

1.2.5. *Program*

An algorithm can be translated, using a programming language, into a sequence of instructions or a program that can be executed by a computer. For human beings, writing sequences of 0 and 1 is not much fun, not very readable, and can lead to many errors. We have therefore invented increasingly advanced programming languages, some quite general, others more adapted to specific fields. The program, written in such a language, will be translated by a program called a compiler in the language known by the machine.

A program represents an algorithm. It is a sequence of instructions defined in a given language and intended to be executed by a computer. This language has, like any language, its alphabet, its words, its grammar and its rules. We will come back to programs and programming languages in Chapter 3.

1.3. Towards automation of calculations

For millennia, humans have used their fingers, stones or sticks to calculate. Then, more sophisticated tools appeared: the use of counting frames (trays on which stones or tokens are moved) or the abacus (Middle East, Russia and China).

Numerous scientific contributions, in particular mathematical and technical, have made it possible to build and use machines designed to calculate more easily, more quickly and, in general, reducing the risk of error. These machines became computers, able to solve very different problems, from network gaming to virtual reality and databases.

Here are a few steps that have marked the progression towards certain automation of calculations and tasks to be performed in different contexts.

1.3.1. *Slide rule*

William Oughtred (1574–1660) developed a slide rule which – by simple longitudinal displacement of graduated scales according to the property of logarithmic functions – enabled the transformation of a product into a sum and a division into a difference, to directly perform arithmetic operations of multiplication and division, and which can also be used to perform more complex operations such as the calculation of square roots, cubic, logarithmic or trigonometric calculations.

Its reign lasted until the mid-1980s, and it was used by many students and engineers until the appearance of pocket calculators.

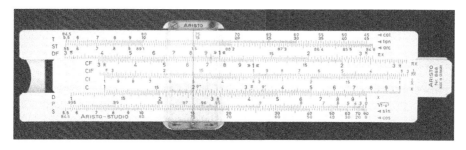

Figure 1.3. *A slide rule (source: Roger McLassus). For a color version of this figure, see www.iste.co.uk/delhaye/computing.zip*

1.3.2. *The Pascaline*

Due to the increase in trade and commerce, people needed more efficient tools to facilitate and, above all, speed up calculations related to commercial transactions. The road to automation was open, and calculators that could progressively automate arithmetic operations were developed.

Figure 1.4. *A Pascaline (source: David Monniaux). For a color version of this figure, see www.iste.co.uk/delhaye/computing.zip*

In 1642, Blaise Pascal (1623–1662) made the first calculator that allowed additions and subtractions to be made by a system of toothed wheels (a gear made it possible to make a deduction). It was perfected by Leibnitz (1694), who afforded it the ability to carry out multiplications and divisions (by successive additions or subtractions).

The Pascaline was at the origin of many machines, as well as key inventions of the industry.

1.3.3. *The Jacquard loom*

While, for centuries, human beings have had the ambition to calculate and then to automate calculations, at the dawn of the Industrial Revolution of the 19th century, they also had the ambition to automate tasks. Falcon (a weaver mechanic) used punched cards in the loom around 1750. But Jacquard (1752–1834) industrialized the invention in 1781. In an endless movement, a series of punched cards attached to each other were passed in front of needles and thus allowed a precise weaving. The punched cards guided the hooks that lift the warp threads, thus enabling complex patterns to be woven. This is an early application of the aforementioned concept of the program. Simple to install, the Jacquard loom spread rapidly throughout Europe. In Lyon, the Jacquard loom was not well received by silk workers (the Canuts) who saw it as a possible cause of unemployment. This led to the Canuts' revolt, during which the workers destroyed machines.

1.3.4. *Babbage's machine*

In 1833, the British mathematician Charles Babbage (1791–1871), who was passionate about Jacquard's work, proposed a very advanced mechanical calculator: the analytical machine. It was a programmable mechanical calculator that used punched cards for its data and instructions, but the machine was never completed. Mathematician Ada Lovelace[2],

---

2 Ada Lovelace (1815–1852) was an English scientist who anticipated the potential of the analytical machine and proposed numerous applications for it. She was the first to formalize the principle of programming, making her first "coder" in history. It is in her honor and for the importance of her work that a programming language, designed between 1977 and 1983 for the US Department of Defense, received the name ADA in 1978.

colleague of Charles Babbage, designed a series of programs (sequences of punched cards) for this machine.

1.3.5. *The first desktop calculators*

The German mathematician Gottfried von Leibnitz (1646–1716) built a more sophisticated machine than the Pascaline, without any real success. Based on this model, in 1820 the Frenchman Thomas de Colmar (1785–1870) invented the arithmometer, a practical, portable and easy-to-use machine. It was an entirely mechanical calculator capable of performing the four operations of arithmetic (addition, subtraction, multiplication and division). It was the first calculator produced in series and marketed (between 1851 and 1915) with great success (more than 1,500 calculators were sold in France).

At the end of the 19th and beginning of the 20th century, there was an explosion of innovations in office machines, all of which were aimed at making them easier to use thanks to an increase in the proportion of automated systems.

The Curta mechanical calculator, invented by the Austrian engineer Curt Herzstark, was produced between 1948 and 1972. Composed of a cylindrical body and a small crank handle, making it look like a pepper mill, it weighed barely 230 grams. It enables the four basic arithmetic operations to be performed very quickly and, after training, other operations such as square roots. My father, who was an astronomer, used a Curta calculator that I could play with!

Figure 1.5. *The Curta mechanical calculator (source: Jean-Marie Hardy).*
For a color version of this figure, see www.iste.co.uk/delhaye/computing.zip

1.3.6. *Hollerith's machine*

In response to a competition launched by the US Census Bureau, Hermann Hollerith (1860–1929) built a punch-card statistical machine that uses cards (12 × 6 cm) with the 210 boxes needed to receive the characteristics of an individual: age, sex, occupation, family situation, etc. The machine was designed to be used for the purpose of collecting data on the characteristics of individuals. The cards are read by an electric reader; a hole lets the current pass through and the absence of a hole stops it.

Not only did Hollerith propose to collect the census data of each inhabitant in this form, but, in addition, he designed a machine that allowed for the automatic processing of these punched cards, the machine adding these data together to produce statistics. The 1880 census was processed (manually) in eight years. The census of 1890 was processed in record speed for the time (between six months and a little more than a year, according to sources).

Figure 1.6. *A Hollerith machine (source: IBM archives)*

Hollerith left the administration and founded the Tabulating Machine Company in 1896 (later, the Computing-Tabulating-Recording Company, CTR), with Thomas J. Watson as director in 1914. In 1924, the company became International Business Machines Corporation, better known as IBM.

In 1924, Fredrik Bull, a Norwegian engineer, filed a patent on a system similar to the Hollerith system. His patents were sold to the French company, *Compagnie des Machines Bull*, founded in 1930 for the purpose of exploiting these patents.

1.4. The first programmable computers

How can we avoid turning the crank handle, as we had to do with the Curta machine, to make a calculation? It is the machine itself that will carry out this task thanks to a program, after providing it with the data to be processed. Let us discuss the programmable calculator.

In 1854, George Boole (1815–1864) designed the algebra that bears his name and is based on two signs (YES = 1, NO = 0) and three operators (AND, OR, NOT). Boole's algebra came to find many applications in computer science and in the design of electronic circuits.

In 1936, Alan Turing[3] proposed his definition of a **machine**, a major contribution to theoretical computer science. He described an abstract machine to give formal support to the notions of algorithm and effective computation.

Electronic circuits, vacuum tubes, capacitors and electronic relays replaced their mechanical equivalents, and numerical computation (using numbers or numerical symbols) replaced analog calculation (using continuous physical measurements, of mechanical or electrical origin) to model a problem. Below are three examples.

1.4.1. *Konrad Zuse's machines*

Konrad Zuse (1910–1995) was a German engineer who was one of the pioneers of programmable calculation, which prefigured computer science.

3 Alan Turing (1912–1954), a British mathematician, is considered one of the fathers of computer science. In 1936, he presented an experiment that would later be called "Turing's machine" and which would give a definition to the concept of algorithm and mechanical procedure. During World War II, he joined the British Secret Service and succeeded in breaking the secrets of German communications and the Enigma machine. After the war, he worked on one of the very first computers and then contributed to the debate on the possibility of artificial intelligence.

He built several machines, but his greatest achievement was the creation of the first programmable binary floating-point electromechanical calculator, the Z3. Started in 1937, it was completed in 1941; it consisted of 2,000 electromechanical relays.

1.4.2. *Colossus*

Colossus was the first electronic calculator based on the binary system. It was developed in London during World War II (1943). It was a calculator specialized for decrypting the Lorenz code, a secret code the Germans reserved for highly important communications during the war. Colossus, an electronic machine programmable using a wiring board, was made up first of 1,500 and then of 2,400 vacuum tubes and performed 5,000 operations per second.

1.4.3. *ENIAC*

The first known programmable electronic digital computer, the ENIAC (Electronic Numerical Integrator and Computer) was developed during World War II at the University of Pennsylvania by Americans John P. Eckert and John W. Mauchly. It went into operation in 1946.

Physically, the ENIAC was a big machine: it contained 17,468 vacuum tubes, 7,200 crystal diodes, 1,500 relays, 70,000 resistors, 10,000 capacitors and about 5 million hand-made welds. It weighed 30 tons, occupying an area of 167 m^2! ENIAC suffered from the unreliability of its components, which comes as no surprise.

ENIAC made its calculations in the decimal system and could be reprogrammed to solve, in principle, all computational problems.

Programming the ENIAC consisted of wiring connections and adjusting electrical buttons, long and complex operations. It became clear that if it was to be used as a flexible machine, capable of a wide variety of calculations, another form of programming was needed.

1.5. Generations of computers

The automation of calculations was therefore progressing well, but the programming of these machines remained a real problem to which a solution needed to be found. This was the arrival of the first computers, whose program can be stored in the memory of the machine itself. And the evolution of computers has proven spectacular.

The first computers date back to 1949. It was the idea, in 1945, of a recorded program, from the Hungarian–American mathematician and physicist John von Neumann[4] and his collaborators, which transformed a calculator into a computer using a unique storage structure to store both the instructions and the data requested or produced by the calculation.

Von Neumann's architecture breaks down the computer into four distinct parts:

– a **calculating organ**, capable of executing arithmetic and logical operations, the arithmetic and logic unit;

– a **central memory**, used both to hold the programs describing how to arrive at the results and the data to be processed;

– **input–output organs** serving as organs of communication with the environment and with the human;

– a **control unit** to ensure consistent operation of the above elements.

The first innovation is the separation between the control unit, which organizes the instruction sequencing flow, and the arithmetic and logic unit, in charge of the execution of these instructions. The second fundamental innovation was the idea of the stored program: instead of being encoded on an external support (tape, cards, wiring board), the instructions are stored in the memory.

A memory location can contain both instructions and data, and a major consequence is that a program can be treated as data by other programs.

---

4 An engineering mathematician, John von Neumann (1903–1957) participated in the development of set theory and was a precursor of artificial intelligence and cognitive science. He also participated in American military programs. He provided decisive impetus to the development of computer science by establishing the principles that still govern computer architecture today.

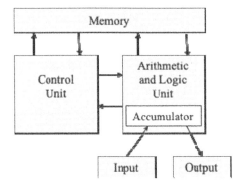

Figure 1.7. *von Neumann's architecture*

The unit formed by the arithmetic and logic unit, on the one hand, and the control unit, on the other hand, constitutes the Central Processing Unit (CPU) or processor. The processor executes the programs loaded into the central memory by extracting their instructions one after the other, analyzing and executing them. All of the physical components, known as hardware, are controlled by software.

Computer calculations are cadenced by a clock whose frequency is measured in hertz. The higher the frequency (and therefore the shorter the basic cycle time), the more operations the computer will be able to perform per second.

The architecture (organization) of computers has evolved and become more complex over the years. Generations of computers are distinguished by the technologies used in the physical components and by the evolution of the software, in particular the operating system, which is the set of programs controlling the various components (processor, memory, peripheral units, etc.) of the computer, thus allowing it to function. The evolution of software is discussed in Chapter 3.

1.5.1. *First generation: the transition to electronics*

From 1948 onwards, the first von Neumann architecture machines appeared: unlike all previous machines, programs were stored in the same memory as data and could therefore be manipulated as data. This is what the aforementioned compiler does: transforms a program describing an algorithm into a machine-readable program.

The first generation is that of electronic tube machines and electromechanical relays.

1.5.1.1. *EDVAC (Electronic Discrete Variable Automatic Computer)*

The design of a new machine, more flexible and, above all, more easily programmable than the ENIAC, had already begun in 1944, before the ENIAC was operational. The design of the EDVAC, to which von Neumann made a major contribution, attempted to solve some of the problems posed by ENIAC's architecture. Like ENIAC, EDVAC was designed by the University of Pennsylvania to meet the needs of the US Army Ballistics Research Laboratory.

The computer was built to operate in binary with automatic addition, subtraction and multiplication, and programmable division, all with automated control and a memory capacity of 1,000 words of 44 bits. It had nearly 6,000 vacuum tubes and 12,000 diodes, consumed 56 kW, occupied an area of 45.5 m^2 and weighed 7,850 kg. It calculated 350 multiplications per second and was released in 1949.

Its plans, which were widely disseminated, gave rise to several other computer projects in the late 1940s and up to 1953.

1.5.1.2. *Harvard Mark III (1949) and IV (1952)*

Designed by Howard H. Aiken (Harvard University), the Harvard Mark III and IV models are among the first registered-program computers. The Mark III, partly electronic and partly electromechanical, was delivered to the US Navy in 1950. The Mark IV, one of the first fully electronic computers, was designed for the Air Force and delivered in 1952.

1.5.1.3. *UNIVAC I (Universal Automatic Computer I)*

The UNIVAC I was the first commercial computer made in the United States. It used 5,200 vacuum tubes, weighed 13 tons, consumed 125 kW for a computing power of 1,905 operations per second with a 2.25 MHz clock. The first computer equipped with magnetic tape units was manufactured by Univac, a subsidiary of the Remington Rand company.

The first copy was completed in 1951, and 46 copies were delivered up to 1958.

1.5.1.4. *IBM 701 and IBM 704*

IBM (International Business Machines Corporation), created in 1924, came to have an essential place in the IT world for many years to come. It developed in the 1930s thanks to the patents of mechanography on the perforated card invented by Hermann Hollerith.

In April 1952, IBM produced its first scientific computer, the IBM 701, for the American Defense Service. The first machine was installed at the Los Alamos (New Mexico) laboratory for the American thermonuclear bomb project, and had two twins designed for commercial applications: the IBM 702 and the IBM 650, of which about 2,000 units were produced until 1962.

In April 1955, IBM launched the IBM 704, scientific computer (its commercial counterpart was the 705). It used a memory with ferrite cores, much more reliable and faster than cathode ray tubes, of 32,768 words of 36 bits. According to IBM, the 704 could execute 40,000 instructions per second.

The 700 series computers, which used electronic components based on electronic tubes, were replaced by the 7000 series, which used transistors.

1.5.2. *Second generation: the era of the transistor*

The transistor was invented in 1947 by Americans John Bardeen, William Shockley and Walter Brattain at Bell Laboratories in New Jersey; they were awarded the Nobel Prize in Physics for this invention in 1956. The transistor represented enormous progress in comparison to electronic tubes: it did the same work as the vacuum lamp of the first computers but, at the same time, was much smaller, lighter and more robust; it also consumed less energy.

Moreover, it worked almost instantaneously once powered up, unlike the electronic tubes, which required about 10 seconds of heating, significant power consumption and a high voltage source (several hundred volts).

This invention had a considerable impact on the design and manufacture of computers.

Figure 1.8. *An electron tube and a transistor (source: public domain photos)*

Transistor-based computers are considered the second generation, and they dominated computing in the late 1950s and early 1960s. Below are a few examples.

1.5.2.1. *Bull Gamma 60*

In 1958, *Compagnie des Machines Bull* (France) announced the Gamma 60, delivered in about 15 units from 1960 onwards. This was the first multitasking computer (capable of running several applications simultaneously) and one of the first to feature several processors. It also included several input and output units: magnetic drums, magnetic strips, card readers, card punches, printers, paper strip readers, paper strip punches and a terminal. Its basic cycle time was 10 µs (microseconds). However, the solid-state computer had design flaws typical of an experimental machine.

1.5.2.2. *IBM 1401*

In 1959, the IBM 1401 appeared, which was the most popular computer system across the world at the beginning of the 1960s. Several factors accounted for this success: it was one of the first computers to operate solely with transistors – instead of vacuum tubes – which made it possible to reduce its size and extend its lifespan; available for rental for $2,500 per month, it was recognized as the first affordable general-purpose computer. Furthermore, the IBM 1401 was also the easiest computer to program at the time.

The 1401 performed 193,000 8-digit additions per minute, and its card reader read 800 cards per minute. It could be equipped with magnetic strips reading an average of 15,000 characters per second. The printer launched with the series produced 600 lines of 132 characters per minute.

Manufactured from 1959 to 1965, it was the best-selling computer of the so-called second-generation computers (more than 10,000 sold).

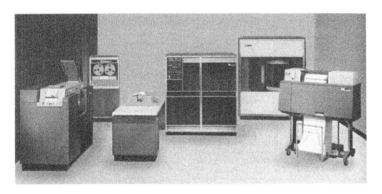

Figure 1.9. *IBM 1401 (source: IBM 1401 Data Processing System Reference Manual)*

1.5.2.3. *IBM 1620*

In 1960, IBM launched the 1620 (scientific) system with different configurations to suit customer needs. There were two models that differed in the cycle time of their memories: 10 µs and 20 µs. Its attractive cost enabled many universities to acquire it, and many students were able to discover computer science thanks to it. About 2,000 units were sold up until 1970.

1.5.2.4. *DEC PDP-1*

In 1960, Digital Equipment Corporation (DEC) launched the PDP-1 (Programmed Data Processor). The PDP-1 was the first interactive computer (allowing easy exchange between the user and the computer) and introduced the concept of the mini-computer. It had a clock speed of 0.2 MHz (cycle time 5 µs) and could store 4,096 18-bit words. It could perform 100,000 operations per second. Fifty examples were built.

1.5.3. *Third generation: the era of integrated circuits*

The invention of the transistor quickly called for the development of a technology that would allow the integration of the computer's different components, because the multiple electrical connections that need to be made between each transistor are complex, expensive to make, not fast enough and not reliable enough.

The first important development with the appearance of the transistor was to mount these transistors on the same circuit board and etch the wires that connected them in the board; the result was known as a printed circuit board. The invention of the printed circuit was attributed to the Frenchman Robert Kapp (1894–1965).

Printed circuits then allowed the invention of the integrated circuit (also called electronic chip), capable of connecting all the elements of the circuit (transistors, diodes, capacitors, wires, etc.) in so-called fully integrated circuits, manufactured in a single operation. The first integrated circuit was invented in 1958 by the American Jack Kilby (1923–2005) while working for Texas Instruments.

Many computers based on these technologies appeared between 1963 and 1971.

1.5.3.1. *IBM/360 and IBM/370*

The creation of the IBM/360 in 1964 was a turning point in the technical history of computing. Taking advantage of the considerable progress in semiconductor technology, IBM researched and brought to market a range of machines with a large number of innovations. The two lines of IBM production, scientific and commercial, met in the IBM/360 series; the choice of the name 360 reflected the desire to cover the entire horizon of computer applications. The 360 series offered a unique machine architecture, from the smallest (360/20) to the most powerful (360/195), in order to facilitate the changes from one model to a larger one. The smallest computer in the family could make 33,000 additions per second and the largest 2,500,000. The series was equipped with various peripherals, including removable hard disk storage units.

Figure 1.10. *IBM/360 computer (source: IBM archives). For a color*
version of this figure, see www.iste.co.uk/delhaye/computing.zip

The 360 series was followed by the 370 series, announced in 1970. It generalized the virtual memory mechanism and brought significant improvement in processor performance, the basic cycle of the 370/195 being 54 nanoseconds. Marketing of this series was stopped in 1983.

Marketed between 1965 and 1978, for both commercial and scientific applications, more than 14,000 units of this range were sold.

Other manufacturers offered systems compatible with these series, especially Japanese manufacturers (Fujitsu, Hitachi).

IBM dominated the world market by a wide margin in the 1960s, and the reference appeared: "IBM and the 7 dwarves", when referring to the 7 competitors of the undisputed leader: Burroughs, Univac, NCR, Control Data Corporation, Honeywell, RCA and General Electric.

1.5.3.2. *CDC 6600*

Control Data occupies a special place in the market of computers dedicated to scientific computing.

Control Data Corporation was a pioneering American company in the manufacture of supercomputers. It was founded in 1957 in Minneapolis-Saint Paul, MN, by American scientists from US Navy research centers, including William Norris and Seymour Cray, who founded Cray Research in 1972. CDC initially focused on computer peripheral units (magnetic tape drives, in particular) before embarking on the construction of computers under the impetus of Seymour Cray.

After the 3600, the first CDC 6600 system was introduced in 1964. At that time, it was 10 times faster than the others. The CDC 6600 was equipped with a transistor CPU with a clock frequency of 10 MHz and had a computing power of 1 Mflops (million floating-point operations per second). This measure of performance in scientific computing was set to continue.

More than 100 units were sold for $8,000,000. This computer is considered to be the first **supercomputer** ever marketed. It was the most powerful computer between 1964 and 1969 when it was surpassed by its successor, the CDC 7600.

In the late 1970s, Control Data developed the CDC Cyber series, marking a significant improvement in performance, but it was too late to take on the Cray-1, the first supercomputer designed entirely by Seymour Cray.

1.5.3.3. *Minicomputers*

Until now, computers were mainly developed for and at the request of the military and the major laboratories associated with them. Their cost, both in purchase and in operation, was very high. But the demand from companies and laboratories of all sizes and from the banking sector was pressing: the market for smaller, easier-to-use, less expensive computers pushed manufacturers to diversify their offer.

The minicomputer was an innovation of the 1970s that became significant towards the end of the decade. It brought the computer to smaller or decentralized structures, not only by taking up less space, reducing costs (acquisition and operation) and providing a degree of independence from large IT service providers, but also by expanding the number of computer manufacturers and thus promoting competition. This range of computers has virtually disappeared due to the rise of personal computers.

In the 1980s, Digital Equipment Corporation (DEC) became the second-largest computer manufacturer (after IBM) with its popular PDP computers (especially the PDP-11, DEC's first machine to use 16-bit rather than 12-bit memory). The PDP series was replaced by the VAX (Virtual Address eXtension), which brought the convenience of the VMS (Virtual Memory System) operating system and was a great success. DEC disappeared in 1998.

Figure 1.11. *A PDP-8 computer (source: Alkivar, Wikipedia). For a color version of this figure, see www.iste.co.uk/delhaye/computing.zip*

The Mitra 15 was one of the computers produced by the Compagnie Internationale pour l'Informatique (CII) as part of the Plan Calcul, a French government plan launched in 1966 to ensure the country's autonomy in information technology. Marketed from 1971 to 1985, it was widely used in higher education and research, as well as for industrial process control and network management. It was also used in secondary education as early as the mid-1970s and was able to operate in conjunction with a large system. A total of more than 7,000 copies were produced.

The Mini 6 was successfully marketed in Europe by the Honeywell-Bull Group from 1976. The Mini 6 was renamed DPS-6 in 1982.

In 1972, Hewlett-Packard launched the HP 3000, a real-time, multi-user, multitasking minicomputer for business applications. At the end of 1980, machines using the HP PA-RISC processor were delivered in large numbers, enabling 32-bit addressing.

In the 1970s, IBM released a series of minicomputers, the 3 series, and then, in the 1980s, the 30 series, which was followed by the AS/400 series that was a great success for management applications (more than 400,000 copies sold).

1.5.4. *Fourth generation: the era of microprocessors*

One definition, not universally accepted, associates the term "fourth generation" with the invention of the microprocessor.

In 1971, the American company Intel succeeded, for the first time, in placing all the components that make up a processor on a single integrated circuit, thus giving rise to the microprocessor.

The first commercially available (still 4-bit) microprocessor, the Intel 4004, was later expanded to 8 bits under the name Intel 8008. These processors were the precursors of the Intel 8080 and the future Intel x86 processor family.

Figure 1.12. *Intel 4040 (source: Konstantin Lanzet collection)*

Its arrival has led to many advances, such as increased operating speed (distances between components are reduced), increased reliability (less risk of losing connections between components), reduced energy consumption, but above all the development of much smaller computers: microcomputers.

The main characteristics of a microprocessor are:

– the complexity of its architecture, which is measured by the number of transistors present: the higher the number, the more complex the tasks to be processed can become. Intel's 4004 included 2,300 transistors; the latest processors include several billions;

– the speed of its clock that dictates the pace of work; the base frequency of the Intel Xeon Phi KNL processor is 1.30 GHz, while that of the 4004 was 740 kHz (more than 1,000 times slower!);

– the number of bits it can process (4 at the beginning, 128 in 2011);

– the fineness of the etching to improve performance and density, and reduce consumption and manufacturing costs.

These characteristics changed very quickly, as shown in Table 1.1, which includes some dates.

	Model	Number of transistors	Clock frequency	Fineness of the etching
1971	Intel 4004	2,300	108 kHz	10 microns
1982	Intel 286	134,000	6 MHz	1.5 micron
1993	Intel Pentium	3.1 million	66 MHz	0.8 micron
2001	Intel Xeon	42 million	1.7 GHz	0.18 micron
2008	Intel Core 2 Duo	410 million	2.4 GHz	45 nm
2012	3rd generation Intel Core	1.4 billion	2.9 GHz	22 nm

Table 1.1. *Evolution of Intel processor characteristics (source: Intel)*

In 2019, Intel officially kicked off its generation of 10 nm processors and the stacking of the different layers of the processor in a 3D design. But the improvement of these features may have limits, which I will discuss further with the race for performance.

Manufacturers Intel and AMD dominate the market for microprocessors, which are found in almost all electronic equipment today.

1.5.4.1. *The invasion of microprocessors*

Today, microprocessors are found in all areas of personal and professional life.

Thanks to tremendous progress in their miniaturization, they are present in our everyday equipment, such as tablets, cell phones, cars, TV sets, game consoles and our bank cards. They are also essential in factories (robots, etc.), in public transportation systems, hospitals, etc.

Some of these areas will be examined in more detail in Chapter 6, on the uses and applications of computer science.

1.5.4.2. *The race for performance*

Regardless of the equipment considered, the performance of the processor(s) in this equipment is an important factor. If my car's ABS system responds late, I am at risk of an accident. If the display on my game console is too slow, I am angry.

Co-founder of the Intel company, Gordon Moore stated, as early as 1965, that the number of transistors per circuit of the same size would double, at constant prices, every year (Moore's law). He later corrected this by increasing the doubling rate to 18 months. He deduced that the power of computers would grow exponentially for years to come. His law, based on an empirical observation, has been verified, even if microprocessor manufacturers now speak of a rate of two years, or even two and a half years.

The increase in performance has therefore been achieved, for a long time, thanks to the evolution of the architecture and the increase in frequency.

Processor architecture has undergone very significant transformations to limit time losses (cycle losses): parallelism in the processors, increase in memory size and hierarchization (e.g. a cache memory integrated in the processor and clocked at the same frequency), etc.

The increase in frequency leads to an increase in the electrical power required, and therefore in the thermal energy generated, which must be dissipated. And the energy consumption of many devices must be controlled, for example, in our smartphones, because it reduces the device's autonomy.

The solution was first found in 2001 with the first multi-core processor: rather than having a single high-frequency processor, for example, two "cores" with lower frequencies were used, each capable of processing instructions individually. This approach became widespread, and by 2018, the most powerful processors had several dozen cores (64 for the Intel Xeon Phi KNL processor, 260 for the Chinese ShenWei SW26010 processor).

Another approach has been to manufacture specialized microprocessors, that is, adapted to a specific need and stripped of everything that is not necessary for its specified use. We have therefore developed coprocessors, electronic circuits designed to add a function to a conventional processor, graphics processors or GPUs (Graphics Processing Unit), FPGAs (Field-Programmable Gate Array), reprogrammable silicon integrated circuits, etc.

1.5.4.3. *Microcomputers*

Consumer microcomputers, or personal computers, appeared in the late 1970s, when the size and cost of a computer allowed an individual to acquire his/her own computer.

Apple's Apple II, Tandy's TRS-80 and Commodore's PET were introduced in 1977.

The 1980s saw the multiplication of microcomputers; many American, European and Asian companies rushed into this new market.

The first commercial success was the IBM PC (1981), equipped with an Intel processor, whose descendants and PC-compatible products (often manufactured in Asia) still largely dominate the market. IBM abandoned this niche in the highly competitive microcomputer market in 2005 when it sold its PC division to the Chinese manufacturer Lenovo.

The first Apple Macintosh, equipped with a Motorola processor, was launched in 1984. With great novelty, it used a mouse and a graphic interface. In 1998, Apple launched a new all-in-one computer, the iMac. After difficult years, mainly due to the high price of its products, Apple reacted, switching from Motorola processors to PowerPC processors and then to Intel processors, while maintaining an innovative spirit. The best known products today are the MacBook Pro, the MacBook Air and the iMac (updated version).

The performance of microcomputers benefitted from the evolution of processors (especially multi-core architectures). A personal computer today has the same power as the number one supercomputer in 1994!

Worldwide PC shipments in 2017 were estimated at 270 million units (according to Gartner), a number that has been steadily declining since 2012. Competition from tablets and even smartphones is one of the reasons for this decline.

The market is dominated by HP (United States) and Lenovo (China), followed by Dell (United States), all of which market PC-compatible products.

1.6. Supercomputers

In some areas, the demand for performance is extreme and supercomputers are being built for this purpose. A supercomputer is a computer designed to achieve the highest possible performance with the techniques known at the time of its design, particularly with regard to computing speed.

1.6.1. *Some fields of use*

The importance of climate science is becoming increasingly evident. The study of climate evolution and its consequences (warming, floods, droughts, etc.) implies the consideration of many parameters (atmosphere, oceans, pollution linked to human or natural activities, etc.). Models must also be able to use increasingly fine grids (spatial division), and a spatial resolution of around 2 km is targeted. Climatologists are therefore demanding ever more powerful computers.

Petroleum exploration uses large amounts of data from drill holes to model a zone and determine whether that zone should be prospected. The economic stakes are enormous.

The health field needs very powerful computers to, for example, analyze the large quantities of data from neuroimaging to study certain diseases (Alzheimer's, Parkinson's, etc.) or to study the interactions between proteins and drugs. We will discuss this further in Chapter 6.

Many industrial sectors need increasingly accurate models, for example, for the design of a new aircraft (aerodynamics) or the safety of a new car (intensive simulations of cockpit deformation in the event of a frontal or side impact).

The analysis of large datasets (Big Data) also requires very high performance. Japan's seismic sensor network collects 100 TB (1,000 billion bytes) of data per year, which must be processed as quickly as possible if an earthquake is to be predicted. Social networks also collect billions of bytes of data that are complex to analyze due to their diversity, and there are many other examples.

Let us not forget the many basic sciences and military applications.

1.6.2. *History of supercomputers*

Racing for performance requires research and innovations, which are then used in all ranges of computers (just as the innovations in Formula 1 racing cars can be found, at least in part, in everyone's car). So, we are going to focus on this, since I have spent part of my professional life in this environment.

It is worth noting that since 1986, a ranking of the 500 most powerful computers operating in the world has been established and published: the TOP500 (top500.org). The performances indicated in the following sections are the maximum performances obtained on the "Linpack benchmark" (a set of programs designed to compensate for performances that are closer to the real world and that are always lower than theoretical performances).

1.6.2.1. *The pioneer: Control Data Corporation*

The first supercomputer is considered to be the CDC 6600, delivered in 1964, which I introduced in the third-generation computers (section 1.5.3.2). The 1970s did see an evolution of the architecture of the CDC 6600/7600 and the creation of the complete range of CDC Cyber systems. The Cyber 205 marked a clear improvement in performance (200 Mflops, or 200 million floating-point operations per second). It was the most powerful computer of its time, but the Cray-1 took its place in a very narrow market that Control Data abandoned to concentrate on other activities.

1.6.2.2. *The Cray saga*

In 1976, the Cray-1 was developed by Seymour Cray, an American scientist who made supercomputer history. It was one of the first computers to use vector processors, applying the same instruction to a consecutive series of operands (thus avoiding repeated decoding times). The Cray-1 was equipped with a single 64-bit processor, developed in-house by Cray, running at 83 MHz. It could compute 160 million floating-point operations per second (160 Mflops) and was Freon-cooled. A total of 85 units were sold at about $5 million each.

In 1982, the Cray XMP was released with two, then four 105 MHz processors, each with a peak performance of 200 Mflops. It was an undeniable success: 189 units were built before 1988. It was replaced by the Cray YMP, which was less successful.

Figure 1.13. *Cray-XMP (source: NSA Photo Gallery). For a color version of this figure, see www.iste.co.uk/delhaye/computing.zip*

1985 saw the marketing of the Cray-2, the first computer to exceed the power of 1.7 Gflops (1.7 billion floating-point calculations per second). The machine was equipped with four processors operating at 250 MHz and had a total power of 1.9 Gflops.

In 1993, Cray produced the T3D that could be equipped with 2,048 processors and reach 300 Gflops. This was a major shift towards massively parallel architectures. It was replaced by the T3E series in 1996.

The Cray-3 was a failure and led the company to bankruptcy; it was sold to Silicon Graphics, which resold this division in 2002 to a young company, Tera Computer, which then took over the Cray name. The Cray saga was thus able to continue!

1.6.2.3. *The arrival of Japanese manufacturers*

Three Japanese manufacturers took their place in this rather closed circle: Hitachi, NEC, but especially Fujitsu.

Hitachi was number 1 in the 1996 TOP500 with CP-PACS/2048. The company has maintained its presence in this market while taking an increasingly smaller share. There were no Hitachi machines in the June 2019 TOP500.

In 1983, NEC introduced the SX-2, which was also a vector computer. It had a power of 1 Gflops. The SX series continued to grow while remaining faithful to the vector architecture for its processors. The latest addition, the SX-9 has a maximum power of 839 Tflops for 8,192 processors.

In 1990, Fujitsu's VP-2600 could reach 5 Gflops with a single processor. Fujitsu built other systems, still ranked among the world's top performers, but had a limited place in this market.

1.6.2.4. *Microprocessors and massive parallelism*

Early supercomputers used "homemade processors", which were very expensive to develop and manufacture. Parallel architectures have given rise to different approaches, based on a very large number of processors, often available "off-the-shelf" and therefore inexpensive since they are produced in very large quantities for various ranges of computers.

Several companies have been created to offer massively parallel systems. One has retained the CM series (Connection Machine) of the Thinking Machine Corporation created in 1983. In its maximum configuration, the CM-5 was announced with a theoretical performance of 2 Tflops, but this efficiency was very dependent on the type of application. The complexity of programming and the reliability of these systems were fatal to these manufacturers (TMC disappeared in 1994). The major manufacturers adopted these massively parallel architectures to base their high-performance systems.

Built in 1997, ASCI Red (built by IBM for Sandia National Lab) was the first supercomputer based on "off-the-shelf" processors to take the lead in the world competition (it stayed there for four years!). In its latest version, it used 9,298 Pentium II Xeon processors with a maximum performance of 3.1 Tflops. It was stopped in 2006.

In 2004, IBM unveiled the Blue Gene/L machine, a series that would lead the competition until 2008. The latest version included more than 100,000 compute nodes for a peak performance of nearly 500 Tflops. The Roadrunner machine, built for the Los Alamos National Laboratory, followed with 20,000 hybrid PowerPC/AMD Opteron CPUs and was the first system to break the 1 Pflops barrier (peta: 10^{15}). IBM then used, for the top end, the Power processors developed in-house.

In 2009, Cray made a strong comeback and became number one with the Jaguar XK6 machine installed at Oak Ridge National Laboratory (1.8 Pflops), which was replaced by the XK7 Titan in 2012 (more than 17 Pflops, with 18,688 AMD Opteron processors and 18,688 Nvidia GPU accelerating the high-performance computing applications).

In November 2010, the French record was held by Bull's TERA-100, installed at CEA. With 17,296 Intel Xeon processors and a performance of 1 Pflops, this machine climbed to sixth place in the world and won first place in Europe. In 2018, TERA-1000 had a theoretical performance of 23 Pflops and was in 16th position.

Figure 1.14. *The IBM Summit machine (source: Oak Ridge National Laboratory)*

In November 2019, IBM was the manufacturer of the two most powerful systems in the world. The first contained 244,000 computing cores, consumed more than 10 MW of energy and could perform 148 million billion calculations in 1 second.

1.6.2.5. *China, a major player since 2010*

Starting in 2010, Chinese manufacturers arrived on the scene and petaflop-scale systems multiplied. In the 2019 TOP500, Lenovo PCs (remember that Lenovo acquired IBM's PC division) accounted for 35% of the top 500 computers, but only 19% of the total installed power. Indeed, the Americans, IBM and Cray, resisted on the very high end.

In 2010, the Chinese Tianhe-1A system led the TOP500 (2.5 Pflops, 14,336 Intel Xeon CPUs and 7,168 GPUs). In 2013, the Chinese Tianhe-2 machine took the lead and stayed there for three years in a row. It was an assembly with 32,000 Intel Ivy Bridge CPUs and 48,000 Intel Xeon Phi for a total of more than 3 million cores and provided 33 Pflops. In 2016, the TaihuLight was the leading system with 41,000 Chinese ShenWei processors (260 cores per processor). It was approaching the 100 Pflops mark. In November 2019, Chinese systems occupied places 3 and 4 in the TOP500.

1.6.3. *Towards exaflops*

In 53 years, maximum performance has increased from 3 Mflops to 93 Pflops, a multiplying factor of 30 billion. Scientific and technological work continues, and the objective is now to reach 1 exaflop (1 billion billion operations per second). But things are not simple!

1.6.3.1. *Challenges for current technologies*

The first challenge is that of energy consumption. We have already said that this consumption concerns (to varying degrees) all electro-technical equipment. But with hundreds of thousands of processors, the problem becomes critical because you cannot build a nuclear power plant to run a supercomputer! The supercomputing community has admitted that the limit of consumption should be 20–30 megawatts, which is already considerable.

How to get there? Three areas are examined:

– hardware: transistor consumption, processor architecture (in particular, associated with specialized processors such as GPUs), memory (capacity and access time), interconnection technologies, etc.;

– software: operating systems that take consumption into account, new programming environments that make parallelism more efficient, data management, new programming environments for the scientists, etc.;

– algorithms: reformulating scientific problems for exaflop-scale systems, facilitating mathematical optimization, etc.

1.6.3.2. *Major ongoing programs*

Given what is at stake, the main countries concerned are releasing considerable budgets to achieve exascale at the beginning of this new decade.

The United States, China and Japan plan to have at least one operational system by 2023. Investment in research and development is estimated at more than $1 billion per year, supported by governments and manufacturers. In August 2019, the US Department of Energy (DoE) announced the signing of a $600 million contract with Cray to install a system with a performance of more than 1 exaflop in 2022. It will be mainly intended for research on nuclear weapons.

No single country in the European Union can muster the scientific, technical and financial resources necessary to compete with Chinese or American efforts. Thus a European program is needed that involves various countries to provide the bulk of the funding and is strongly supported by the European Commission through the PRACE (Partnership for Advanced Computing in Europe) and ETP4HPC (European Technology Platform for High Performance Computing) initiatives. The aim is to have an operational system by 2023–2024, equipped with technologies that are largely European (ARM, Bull). To this end, on January 11, 2018, the European Commission announced the launch of the EuroHPC program, with initial funding of about 1 billion euros between 2018 and 2020, and a second round of funding of about 4 billion euros expected to be provided from 2021 onwards.

In all of these projects, the cost of acquiring a system would be between $300 and $400 million.

1.7. What about the future?

Then, the current technology will be at the end of its possibilities, at least to reach very high performance, and new technologies will have to be found. When will this happen? And with what constraints and consequences?

1.7.1. *An energy and ecological challenge*

The electricity consumption of the 14 billion computers, game consoles, set-top boxes and Internet boxes represented 616 TWh globally in 2013[5].

The world's data centers account for 4% of global energy consumption, half of which is related to cooling and air-conditioning. A large data center consumes as much energy as a French city of 100,000 inhabitants.

Google is said to have more than 1 million servers in more than 10 data centers around the world. The locations are chosen according to the cooling possibilities of the machines (cold regions, proximity to vast reserves of cold water). Google has been working for a long time on the energy efficiency of its data centers and announced, in the midst of COP21, the purchase of 842 megawatts of renewable energy for its data centers, with the long-term aim of relying 100% on clean energy for its activities.

Let us not forget the consumption of cell phones and other computerized objects, produced in the billions, which use phenomenal quantities of batteries, most of which end up in landfill. Some estimate that computing (computers, networks, etc.) consumes nearly 10% of the world's electricity consumption.

Energy consumption is not the only issue we need to consider. The materials used in computers, telephones and other objects are not neutral: various metals, elements of the rare earth family (lanthanides), whose access is considered particularly critical by international bodies, have become strategic issues. High-tech products require rare metals whose production is controlled by a limited number of countries, mainly China, Russia, the Democratic Republic of Congo, and Brazil. The scarcity and weakness of recycling can become very strong industrial and ecological constraints.

---

5 Source: planetoscope.com.

1.7.2. *Revolutions in sight?*

Research on totally different technologies is multiplying, both in laboratories and with processor manufacturers.

Quantum computers are the equivalent of classical computers but can perform calculations directly using the laws of quantum physics. Unlike a classical transistor-based computer that works on binary data (encoded on bits, worth 0 or 1), the quantum computer works on qubits whose quantum state can have several values. Quantum computers are so complex that they are not intended for the general public. They are useful only for very specific applications. The main practical application for a quantum computer today is cryptography.

Neuromorphic processors, inspired by the brain, are another major line of research in an attempt to create the computing power of tomorrow. They are capable of responding to the increasing computing power required by, among other things, artificial intelligence, Big Data, research in chemistry, materials science, and molecular modeling. At the end of 2017, Intel unveiled a chip called Loihi, whose architecture is inspired by the way the human brain functions, with interactions between thousands of neurons. This technology would be well suited to applications based on artificial intelligence.

Other avenues are being explored, such as the optical computer (or photonic computer), a digital computer that uses photons for information processing, while conventional computers use electrons. Other approaches exist that are essentially secret because they are studied in research laboratories.

Readers interested in this research can immerse themselves in the specialized literature.

2

Computer Networks and
Their Applications

2.1. Introduction

Communication is an essential aspect of life for all species, both within (human to human) and between them (human to animal, human to plant, etc.). This communication can concern two actors, one actor and one group, several groups, etc.

We will limit ourselves to communication centered on the transmission of information, as defined in Chapter 1.

Communicating information involves several elements:

– the sender: the entity that sends a message. In this chapter, it will generally be computer equipment;

– the receiver(s): the entity/entities receiving the message;

– the message: an element that carries information of any kind. This message is transmitted from the sender to the receiver(s);

– the channel: the path through which the message will circulate, between the transmitter and the receiver. This channel can be a cable, the air, etc.;

– the code: the language in which the message is formulated. This language must be understandable, or translated to be understandable by the receiver;

– a protocol: this ensures the correct organization of the transmission. In a telephone conversation, not everyone speaks at the same time;

– other elements such as the identification of the actors, confidentiality conditions, etc.

We are entering a complex world of hardware, algorithms, software, conventions, etc., and we have to deal with a lot of different things. This world fascinates many research teams, whether in universities or telecommunications industries.

After mentioning a few dates that have marked their development, this chapter will approach computer networks from three angles:

– the hardware **infrastructure** that provides the links between the entities constituting the networks;

– the **protocols** that enable the organizing of the communications in regard to these infrastructures;

– the major types of **applications** that we commonly use, leaving more precise descriptions of the use of information technology for Chapter 6.

We will finish on an aspect that concerns us all: security.

2.2. A long history

Computer networks have undergone tremendous development, from the first connection between two machines to cloud computing. We will limit ourselves to the aspects that have structured this development and to those that we may encounter in our activities.

On the basis of what we know today, the first communication systems date back to the 19th century. Here are some key dates:

– 1791: Frenchman Claude Chappe invented the semaphore, also known as the **optical telegraph**. The semaphore makes it possible to send messages quickly over a long distance using, as its infrastructure, a network of towers surmounted by an articulated arm to transmit coded signals on sight;

– 1838: Samuel Morse, an American physicist, developed the system of dots and dashes (we have heard the ti-ta-ta-ti sound in various films!), which is known throughout the world as **Morse code**. In 1844, he sent the first message on a telegraph line between Baltimore and Washington. From 1846, the Morse telegraph was developed by private companies. It is perhaps the first communication system;

Figure 2.1. *Morse code manipulator (source: Musée des Arts and Métiers). For a color version of this figure, see www.iste.co.uk/delhaye/computing.zip*

– 1850: William Thomson (Lord Kelvin), a British physicist, imagined the construction of the first transatlantic cable. Cyrus Field, an American businessman and financier, laid the first **transatlantic telegraph** cable in 1858;

– 1876: Alexander Graham Bell, a Scottish-Canadian scientist, engineer and inventor, filed a patent for the invention of the **telephone**, a system for transmitting voice over electrical wires (although this authorship is controversial). The invention quickly met with resounding success, leading to the creation of the Bell telephone company in 1877;

– 1897: Guglielmo Marconi, an Italian physicist, inventor and businessman, considered one of the inventors of radio, filed patents on **wireless telegraphy**. In 1901, the first wireless telegraphic transmission across the Atlantic was made. The wireless transmission opened up a new era in telecommunications by using the waves for transmission;

– 1906: Canadian Reginald Fessendem invented the **radio** and made the first wireless transmission of speech across the Atlantic in both directions;

– 1907: Frenchman Édouard Belin invented the **belinograph**, a system for the remote transmission of photographs, which was used in the press in the 1930s, until its replacement by the transmission of digital files 50 years later;

– 1925: John Baird, a Scottish engineer, demonstrated the **transmission of moving images**. Baird's device would become known as "mechanical television";

– 1930: the first **telex networks** were set up, with teletypewriters now capable of reproducing text typed on a keyboard automatically and remotely on a typewriter. Telex was used all over the world until the 1990s and gradually disappeared with the arrival of fax machines, computer networks and electronic messaging.

During World War II, the laboratories of the warring parties perfected new applications:

– 1935: the first **radar** network was commissioned by the British. The **walkie-talkie** made its appearance in 1941, in the form of a portable radio transceiver for radio links over short distances;

– 1950s: the model of networks known as **nodes**, connected by links, appeared with the birth of the probabilistic queuing theory;

– 1960: Joseph Licklider, from the Massachusetts Institute of Technology, published the article "Man-Computer Symbiosis", emphasizing the need for simpler interaction between computers. During the Cold War, he worked on the SAGE (Semi-Automatic Ground Environment) project, which was designed to create an air defense system. Designed around a network of computers and numerous radar station sites, this system made it possible to produce, in real time, a unified image of the airspace over the entire US territory and to be able to provide an immediate tactical response in the event of danger. It was operational from 1952 to 1984. SAGE was probably the first **computer network**. This network was adapted to set up a computer reservation system for American Airlines, the SABRE network, which was deployed in the 1960s;

– 1961: Leonard Kleinrock identified a key point that would enable the application of these theories: the concept of a **router**, that is, a node capable of storing a message, while waiting for the link which it is to be retransmitted on, to become free. Routers play an essential role in today's networks;

– 1964: the principle of **packet switching** was published for the first time. Packet switching consists of segmenting information into data packets, transmitted independently by intermediate nodes and reassembled at the receiver level. This is an important advance compared to the previously used circuit switching, which required the reservation of communication resources for the entire duration of the conversation and over a complete path between the two machines involved in the dialogue. We will come back to these switching modes later;

– 1969: the first packet-switched computer network, **ARPAnet**, was launched. It connected four American research laboratories and was developed by DARPA, the technology research agency of the US Department of Defense, in close collaboration with major universities (UCLA, Stanford, etc.);

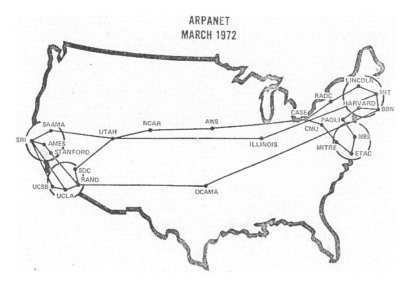

Figure 2.2. *ARPAnet in March 1972 (source: Wikimedia Commons)*

– 1971: creation of Cyclades, an experimental French telecommunications network using packet switching, designed by Louis Pouzin with IRIA (*Institut de recherche en informatique et en automatique*);

– 1974: Americans Vint Cerf and Robert Kahn published a book in which they describe **TCP/IP** (Transmission Control Protocol/Internet Protocol), the protocol that allows heterogeneous networks to communicate with each other;

– 1976: establishment of the **X.25 standard** for packet-switched networks, developed by the CNET (*Centre national d'études des télécommunications*). In 1978, Transpac, a subsidiary of the telecommunications operator France

Télécom, was created to operate the first commercial packet data transmission network in France. The Télétel network used by the Minitels and distributed by France Télécom was based on Transpac's X.25 network. Operation of the X.25 network ended in 2012;

– 1982: creation of the term **Internet**: a set of interconnected networks using the common TCP/IP protocol. ARPAnet officially adopted the TCP/IP standard;

– 1991: invention of the World Wide Web by Tim Berners-Lee, at CERN (European Organization for Nuclear Research, located in Geneva). In the following years, the first navigation software (Mosaïc, Netscape Navigator) and search engines (Yahoo, then Google, etc.) appeared;

– 1992: start of the French network **RENATER** (*Réseau national de communications électroniques pour la technologie, l'enseignement et la recherche*);

– 1990s: development of wired (**ADSL**) or wireless (**Wi-Fi** and **Bluetooth**) broadband networks and mobile Internet (**WAP**);

– 2000+:

- the appearance of **mobile applications** linked to the arrival and democratization of mobile terminals: smartphones, touch tablets, etc.,

- the **Internet of Things** appeared thanks to RFID (Radio Frequency Identification) technology. These connected objects, with their own digital identity, communicate with each other and with people.

2.3. Computer network infrastructure

A computer network is a set of computers that connect to each other and exchange information. In addition to computers, a network can also contain specialized equipment such as modems, hubs, routers and many others that we will discuss in this section.

Computer networks are composed of three elements:

– communication media (cables, optical fibers, radio links, etc.);

– interconnection equipment (nodes, routers, bridges, gateways, etc.);

– terminal equipment (computers, workstations, servers, peripheral devices, etc.).

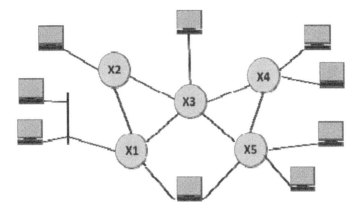

Figure 2.3. *Network diagram with stations and routers. For a color version of this figure, see www.iste.co.uk/delhaye/computing.zip*

There are three important characteristics of network infrastructures:

– **throughput**, which is the amount of information transmitted through a communication channel in a given time interval. The throughput of a connection is generally expressed in bits per second (with the multiples K for thousands, M for millions, G for billions);

– **transmission delay**, which is the time it takes for data to travel from the source to the destination over the network;

– **error rate**, which is the ratio of the number of bits received in error to the total number of bits transmitted.

2.3.1. *Geographic coverage: from PAN to WAN*

Networks can be classified according to their extent, with four very common terms summarizing this extent.

Personal Area Networks (PANs) are restricted networks of computer equipment that are usually for personal use (computer, printer, telephone, etc.).

Local Area Networks (LANs) are mainly intended for local communications, generally within the same entity (company, administration, school, home, etc.), over short distances (a few kilometers maximum). They can connect from two to a few hundred computers with cables or wireless connections. Ethernet LANs are the most common, thanks to the simplicity of their implementation and the gradual increase in connection speeds, from 10 Mbit/s, then 100 Mbit/s, to 1 Gbit/s, then 10 Gbit/s.

Metropolitan Area Networks (MANs) are generally the size of a city and are interconnect networks (LANs or other networks), using dedicated high-speed lines (especially optical fibers).

Wide Area Networks (WANs) interconnect multiple LANs or MANs over large geographic distances, on a national or global scale. The largest WAN is the Internet.

2.3.2. Communication media

To connect two distant forms of computer equipment, a transmission medium is required.

Figure 2.4. *Communication media. For a color version of this figure, see www.iste.co.uk/delhaye/computing.zip*

Communication media can be cables carrying electrical signals, the atmosphere (or space vacuum) where radio waves circulate, or optical fibers that propagate light waves.

These media have quite different characteristics in terms of useful throughput and reliability, and they "cohabit" in today's computer networks according to various conditions and constraints (costs, distances, required throughput, etc.). Here are the most commonly used media.

2.3.2.1. *Copper cables*

The **Public Switched Telephone Network** (PSTN) was the first medium used, because it existed even before computers. On the subscriber's side, the network ends with a pair of copper wires connected to a switch. The telephone connected to it converts the speech signal into an electrical signal. The signal then reaches the switch, which directs it to another subscriber, possibly through other switches. France is planning to shut down its PSTN-type telephone network, but this does not mean the end of fixed telephone service: it will continue to be provided over next-generation networks (voice over IP), copper or fiber.

In order to connect computer equipment and transmit/receive digital data independently of conventional (i.e. analog) telephone services, a **modem** (modulator/demodulator) is used to convert the digital data from the equipment into a modulated signal that can be transmitted over an analog network, and vice versa.

The **Integrated Services Digital Network** (ISDN) is the digital equivalent of the analog telephone network. It uses the same physical infrastructure, but all signals remain in a digital form, making it more convenient for non-voice applications. It is therefore an extension of digital access to the subscriber.

Dedicated telephone lines, that is, telephone lines reserved for this purpose, have become necessary and popular since the 1970s. They make it possible to link several sites of a company, or the university campuses of a city, for example. They were also the basis for interconnecting large networks before fiber optics became essential.

The Power Line Carrier (PLC) has been used for some time, in low speed, for industrial applications and home automation (devices in the home are integrated into systems that need to communicate with each other in order to manage automation). The principle of PLC consists of superimposing a higher-frequency, low-energy signal on the 50 or 60 Hz alternating current. Therefore, existing electrical wiring is used.

The **twisted pair** consists of two insulated copper wires about 1 mm thick. These wires are helically wound, one on top of the other, to reduce the disturbing electromagnetic radiation found in parallel wires. The twisted pair can be used to transmit analog or digital signals and has a bandwidth of several Mbit/s over a few kilometers. Due to its satisfactory performance and low cost, the twisted pair is still widely used.

The coaxial cable is a cable with two conductors of opposite poles separated by an insulating material. The cable consists of a central conductor called the core, usually made of copper, which is embedded in a dielectric insulating material. The core is surrounded by a shield, which acts as a second conductor. In computer networks, the coaxial cable has been gradually replaced by fiber optics (for long-distance use, more than one kilometer) since the end of the 20th century.

Figure 2.5. *Twisted pairs and coaxial cable. For a color version of this figure, see www.iste.co.uk/delhaye/computing.zip*

2.3.2.2. The optical fiber

An optical fiber is a very thin glass or plastic wire that can be a conductor of light and is used in data transmission. By convention, a pulse of light indicates a bit with a value of 1, and the absence of light, a bit with a value of 0. It is increasingly used by operators, in buildings, cities and even in underwater cables, to allow the interconnection of networks worldwide. Its throughput can reach 1 million Gb/s, which is its great advantage.

Figure 2.6. *Fiber optic bundle. For a color version of this figure, see www.iste.co.uk/delhaye/computing.zip*

2.3.2.3. *Wireless transmission*

Cables have a major drawback: they are fixed and do not meet our mobility needs.

A wireless network is a network in which at least two devices can communicate without a wired connection. With wireless networks, a user has the ability to stay connected while traveling within a reasonably large geographical area.

Wireless technologies mainly use electromagnetic waves as a medium. The transmission and reception of these waves is carried out by antennas, integrated in wireless cards. The waves have a defect: they attenuate with the distance they travel and with the obstacles (walls, etc.) they encounter. The use of radio waves for data transmission is becoming increasingly widespread: cell phones, satellite communications, connected objects, etc.

There are several wireless network technologies, differing in the frequency of transmission used and the speed and range of transmissions. The three main standards can be selected according to the geographical area offering connectivity (coverage area): Bluetooth, Wi-Fi and GSM.

Bluetooth is a communication standard that allows the bidirectional exchange of data over very short distances. It has a theoretical data rate of up to 2 Mb/s and a range of 50 m to 100 m. It is often present on devices that operate on battery power and wish to exchange a small amount of data over a short distance: cell phones, laptops and various peripherals (mouse, keyboard, etc.). We are therefore in the field of wireless personal area networks (WPAN).

Wi-Fi is a set of wireless communication protocols governed by the IEEE 802.11 group of standards. With Wi-Fi standards, it is possible to create high-speed wireless local area networks. The range can reach several dozen meters indoors (generally between 20 and 50 meters), if there are no obstructions (concrete walls, for example) between the transmitter and the user. In practice, Wi-Fi makes it possible to connect laptops, office machines, personal digital assistants (PDAs), communicating objects or even peripheral devices, with a very high-speed connection. It is the protocol we use most often in our homes.

GSM (Global System for Mobile Communications) is a digital standard for mobile telephony. The third generation of mobile telephony (3G), whose main standard is UMTS, has made it possible to significantly increase the available bandwidth. Finally, 4G technology is the new generation, which is expanding around the world, with a throughput of up to 1 GB/sec. 5G technology, which is in preparation, will make it possible to download a film in a few seconds and will open up the market to new applications. We are in the field of wireless wide area networks (WWAN).

Even if the main activity of telecommunication satellites is the broadcasting of television programs, they are also used for mobile applications, such as communications to ships or airplanes. However, this could soon change, with operators in many countries launching into the race for mega satellite constellations providing Internet coverage to the entire world from space.

New technologies (e.g. the Loon project launched by Google, which involves deploying Internet coverage to areas that are very difficult to access, via balloons floating at an altitude of 20 kilometers), as well as new uses are being prepared.

2.3.3. *Interconnection equipment and topologies*

2.3.3.1. *Most common equipment*

The **network card** is the most important component. It is indispensable: all the data that needs to be sent and received from a network in a computer passes through it. The **MAC address** (Media Access Control), composed of 12 hexadecimal characters[1], is the physical address of the card, a unique and worldwide address assigned at its manufacture. Your personal computer, smartphone and Wi-Fi box have a MAC address that should not be confused with the address relating to the network (e.g. IP address, which we will discuss in section 2.4.5).

A **repeater** is an electronic device combining a receiver and a transmitter, which compensates for the transmission losses of a medium (line, fiber or radio) by amplifying and possibly processing the signal, without modifying

---

1 Hexadecimal characters are numbers from 0 to 9, and letters from A to F. .

its content. It is used to duplicate and readapt a digital signal, to extend the maximum distance between two nodes in a network.

A **hub** (or **concentrator**) is a piece of hardware that concentrates network traffic from multiple hosts. It has as many ports to connect machines to each other (usually 4, 8, 16 or 32) and acts as a multi-socket to broadcast the information it receives from one port, to all of the other ports. Thus, all the machines connected to the concentrator can communicate with each other.

If the hub is unable to filter the information and transmit it to all the machines connected to it, the **switch** only directs the data to the destination machine based on its address. If computer 1 sends data to computer 2, only computer 2 will receive it.

A **router** is a piece of computer network interconnection equipment used to route data between two or more networks, in order to determine the path that a data packet will take. It is used to connect two different networks. For example, it is the boundary between the local network and the external network (Internet or other).

2.3.3.2. *Some interconnection topologies*

The topology of a network corresponds to its physical architecture. We can retain the following main topologies.

A **bus topology** is the simplest organization of a network. In a bus topology, all computers share a single transmission line (the bus) via a cable, usually coaxial. This is the common topology of an Ethernet-type local area network.

Figure 2.7. *Bus topology*

It has the advantage of being easy to implement and has a simple function. On the other hand, it is very vulnerable because if one of the connections is faulty, the whole network is affected. In addition, the transmission speed is low because the cable is common.

In a **star topology**, the computers in the network are connected to a central hub or switch system. Networks with a star topology are much less vulnerable because one of the connections can be disconnected without crippling the rest of the network. However, communication becomes impossible if the central element is no longer working.

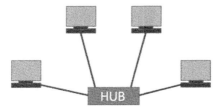

Figure 2.8. *Star topology*

In a **ring network**, all entities are connected together in a closed loop. Data flows in a single direction, from one entity to the next. At any given moment, only one node can transmit on the network and there can be no collision between two messages, unlike the bus-type network. This topology is used by the Token Ring and FDDI networks.

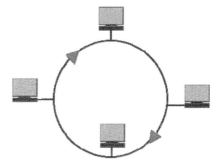

Figure 2.9. *Ring topology*

In a **hierarchical topology**, also called a tree topology, the network is divided into levels. The top is connected to several nodes lower down in the hierarchy. These nodes can themselves be connected to several nodes below them. The weak point of this type of topology is the "parent" computer in the hierarchy, which, if it fails, paralyzes part of the network.

Figure 2.10. *Tree topology*

In a **meshed topology**, each terminal is connected to all of the others. The disadvantage is that the number of connections required becomes very high. Indeed, the number of cables is n (n - 1)/2, if n is the number of computers. For example, it takes 28 cables to interconnect 8 computers, so this topology is used very little.

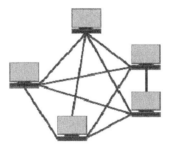

Figure 2.11. *Mesh topology*

Hybrid topologies, combining several different topologies, are the most common. The Internet is an example.

2.3.3.3. *Addressing in networks*

The presence of a multitude of terminal equipment makes it necessary to define a coherent identification system within the network to differentiate them; this is called **addressing**. In addition, the network must be able to route information to any addressee according to their address: this is the **routing** function. When you put a letter in a mailbox, with the recipient's address, this letter will be picked up by an employee of the company in charge of its routing (e.g. the postal service) and transported to a sorting center. Routing operations, sometimes complex, will allow this letter to arrive at the sorting center, in which the recipient is identified by their postal code. Therefore, a destination address and routing system are required. If you add your address on the back of the envelope, the addressee will be able to reply in the same way.

Early computer networks shared the same protocol and namespace. Each computer had a name, and all of the names were collected in tables that were installed on all members of these networks, which allowed routing. In order to communicate with another network, a computer that was a member of both networks had to act as a gateway and translate addresses from one to the other. It was fairly simple because there were only a few thousand computers at most. This is what I experienced in the late 1980s with the interconnection of the IBM and Digital Equipment "worlds" in universities.

The arrival of the Internet and the passage to millions of interconnected devices complicated the situation. Very precise addressing rules were developed little by little. We will discuss this further in section 2.4.4.

2.3.4. *Two other characteristics of computer networks*

2.3.4.1. *Switching technologies*

Switching is necessary when a call is made over several links in succession. Intermediate equipment associates an (inbound) link with another (outbound) link among those available.

In **circuit switching** (analog process), all of the links (the circuit) used for one communication are reserved for that one communication for its entire duration. Its concept and implementation simplicity made it successful in its use in the first communication networks, such as the telephone. It was the responsibility of the operators of a telephone switchboard to establish communications between users in the early decades of the telephone.

In **message switching** (digital process), there is no reservation of resources. A connection is only used by a communication during the periods of transmission of these messages. Messages from other communications can use the same links during this communication. Messages arriving at the switching node are processed in the order of arrival, which can generate queues.

Packet switching (digital process) uses the same principle as message switching, but the messages are made up of a succession of packets, whose size is better suited to the efficiency of the transmission. It is the most commonly used process in networks like the Internet. The problem that needs to be solved is the reassembly of the packets that make up the message.

2.3.4.2. Client–server and peer-to-peer architectures

There are two types of network architecture: client–server and peer-to-peer.

In **client–server** architecture, client machines (machines that are part of the network, such as a personal computer) communicate with a server (usually a powerful machine) that provides services (such as access to files, or a mail server). When the server has responded to the client's request, the connection is terminated. There are countless examples of these communications, such as consulting a train schedule on the railway company server from your personal computer, or your phone. The client/server model has become one of the main concepts in network architectures.

The term **peer-to-peer** is often abbreviated to P2P. In a peer-to-peer system, nodes are simultaneously clients and servers of other nodes on the network, unlike client–server systems. The particularity of peer-to-peer architecture is that data can be transferred directly between two stations connected to the network, without passing through a central server. Peer-to-peer systems therefore facilitate the sharing of information and can be used, for example, for file sharing or distributed computing.

Figure 2.12. *Client–server versus peer-to-peer*

2.3.5. *Quality of service*

Imperfections in telephone conversations are usually not a problem, but this is not the case for data transmission, as the data must arrive at its destination complete and intact. The equipment involved (transmitter, receiver) must ensure this. The quality of service (QoS) of a data circuit is measured using several criteria:

– the error rate (ratio between the number of erroneous bits received and the number of bits transmitted);

– packet loss is the non-delivery of a data packet, mostly due to network congestion;

– availability (proportion of time during which communication is possible);

– the rate (number of bits transmitted per second);

– the response time, which is related to the network throughput and the capacity of the equipment involved in the transmission.

The quality of service is subject to precise technical measurements, but for a user, it is quite subjective because it depends on their expectations and the type of network usage they have at any given time. For example, response time may seem acceptable if the user is looking at bus schedules, but completely unacceptable if they are participating in a videoconference, because it can greatly disrupt the flow of exchanges.

If an operator tells the users that the fiber optic connection in their home provides a speed of several hundred million bits per second, has the response time, in their use of the network, improved significantly compared to the connection they had previously? Not necessarily, because any network transaction involves a lot of intermediate equipment and many network sections with different speeds and congestion rates. The "effective" throughput will therefore depend on many parameters and may vary depending on the period and type of transaction.

2.4. Communication protocols and the Internet

2.4.1. *The first protocols*

Communication media "physically" connect equipment. As in any communication, a method is needed so that two entities can understand each other. A **communication protocol** is a set of rules that define how communication between two entities in a network should take place. Some of the important functions of a protocol include:

– address management (sender and receiver);

– management of the format of the exchanged data;

– routing between different networks;

– detection of transmission errors;

– management of information losses when they occur;

– flow management (the receiver must not be saturated if it is slower than the transmitter).

The protocols are hierarchically **layered**, with each one having to deal with specific functions.

In the 1960s, computing was centralized; that is, data was managed on "mainframes" that could be accessed by remote stations. These computers were linked together by networks operating on the basis of protocols developed by their manufacturers. The two most important protocols of this type are DECnet and SNA.

DECnet is a layered network architecture, based on a protocol defined by the Digital Equipment Corporation, the first version of which, in 1975, allowed two PDP-11 minicomputers to communicate. Large networks of computers from this manufacturer, particularly VAX machines, were deployed until the arrival of TCP/IP protocols.

SNA (Systems Network Architecture) is a layered network architecture defined by IBM in 1974. It is a functional architecture of the same type as the OSI reference model (which it precedes by seven years) and is also part of the IBM product family. Like DECnet, it is a proprietary architecture. SNA has been widely used by computer centers in banks, financial institutions and research centers equipped with IBM hardware.

The major flaw of proprietary architectures, such as those that will come to be cited, is that it is not easy to make them communicate with each other, unless an agreement is reached and a communication protocol is written between these architectures.

2.4.2. *The OSI model*

To solve this problem, in the 1970s, the ISO (International Organization for Standardization) developed a reference model called the OSI (Open Systems Interconnection). This model described the concepts used to standardize the interconnection of systems. It was organized in seven distinct layers, each bearing a number, ranging from the most abstract data (layer number seven) to physical data (layer number one). The OSI standard was published in 1984.

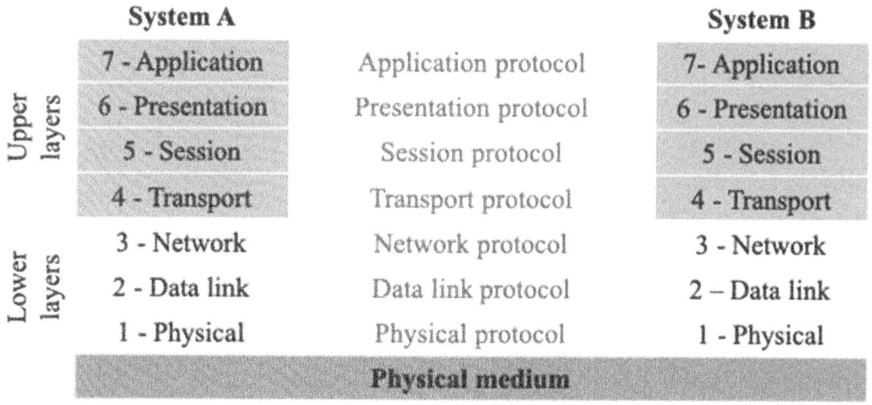

	System A		System B
	7 - Application	Application protocol	**7- Application**
Upper layers	**6 - Presentation**	Presentation protocol	**6 - Presentation**
	5 - Session	Session protocol	**5 - Session**
	4 - Transport	Transport protocol	**4 - Transport**
	3 - Network	Network protocol	3 - Network
Lower layers	2 - Data link	Data link protocol	2 – Data link
	1 - Physical	Physical protocol	1 - Physical
	Physical medium		

Figure 2.13. *The OSI model. For a color version of this figure, see www.iste.co.uk/delhaye/computing.zip*

Let us quickly describe the seven layers:

1) the **physical** layer provides the means to activate, maintain and deactivate the physical connections necessary for the transmission of a groups of bits;

2) the **data link** layer provides the transmission of information between two (or more) immediately adjacent systems and fragments the data into several frames;

3) the **network** layer takes care of routing the data from point A to point B and addressing. The objects exchanged are often called packets;

4) the **transport** layer provides end-to-end data transmission. It maintains a certain transmission quality. Exchanged objects are often called messages (also for the upper layers);

5) the **session** layer provides the means for cooperating entities to synchronize, interrupt or resume their dialogues while ensuring the consistency of the data exchanged;

6) the **presentation** layer is in charge of the representation of the information that the entities exchange. It takes care of semantics, syntax, encryption, deciphering, in short, any "visual" aspect of the information;

7) the **application** layer acts as an interface to provide access to network services. It includes numerous protocols adapted to the different classes of applications (file transfer, e-mail, etc.).

2.4.3. *The history of the Internet*

In the United States, the Defense Advanced Research Projects Agency (DARPA), which is responsible for military defense research projects, launched a computer network project in 1966 linking certain American universities. In 1980, this network, called ARPAnet, became a military issue and was divided into two: the university network became NSFnet, funded by the NSF (National Science Foundation). ARPAnet became the heart of the future Internet and a tool for the development of this new technology.

The NSFnet network opened up to the world, and interconnection problems soon emerged. Communication between networks using different architectures (proprietary or not) became too complex.

Extensive research and development work in 1977, in which the differences between the protocols were blurred by the use of a common communication protocol, led to the demonstration of a prototype, called TCP/IP. On January 1, 1983, TCP/IP officially became the only protocol on ARPAnet. The Internet (from "inter-network"), takes the meaning of a worldwide network using the TCP/IP protocol.

The Internet is not a new type of physical network. It offers, through the interconnection of multiple networks, a global virtual network service based on TCP (Transmission Control Protocol) and IP (Internet Protocol) protocols. This virtual network is based on a global addressing that is placed above the different networks used. The various networks are interconnected by routers. Thanks to the growing interest in vast communication networks and the arrival of new applications, Internet techniques have spread to the rest of the world.

2.4.4. The TCP/IP protocol

The OSI model has been developed with a normative vocation (i.e. to serve as a reference in the course of communication between two hosts), whereas the TCP/IP model has a descriptive vocation (i.e. it describes the way in which communication takes place between two hosts).

TCP/IP actually refers to two closely related protocols: a transmission protocol, TCP (Transmission Control Protocol), which is used over a network protocol, IP (Internet Protocol). It is also a set of protocols that are generally used at the application layer, using TCP/IP.

The TCP/IP model is simpler than the OSI model, with only four layers:

1) the **network** layer includes the physical and data link layers of the OSI model. The only constraint of this layer is to allow a host to send IP packets over the network;

2) the **Internet** layer is the cornerstone of the architecture. Its role is to allow the injection of packets into any network and the routing of these packets, independently of each other, to their destination. The Internet layer has an official implementation: the IP protocol;

3) the **transport** layer has the same role as that of the OSI model: to allow even entities to support a conversation. This layer has a main official implementation: the TCP protocol, a reliable, connection-oriented protocol that allows the error-free routing of packets from one machine on the Internet to another machine on the same Internet;

4) the **application** layer contains all high-level protocols, such as Telnet, SMTP (Simple Mail Transfer Protocol) and HTTP (HyperText Transfer

Protocol). It has indeed been noted with use that network software rarely uses the presentation and session layers of the OSI model.

TCP/IP is an open protocol that is independent of any particular architecture or operating system. This protocol is also independent of the physical medium of the network. This allows TCP/IP to be carried by different media and technologies.

2.4.5. *IP addressing*

Each piece of equipment on a network is identified by an address, called the **IP address**. The addressing mode is common to all TCP/IP users regardless of the platform they use.

The MAC address, already mentioned, is a unique identifier assigned to each network card, but in a large network, there is no central element that knows the location of the recipient and can send the data accordingly. The IP address system, on the other hand, is used in a process called routing to ensure that the data reaches the recipient. Currently, two versions of IP coexist: IPv4 and IPv6.

In IPv4, the addresses are exactly 32 bits (4 bytes): enough to code 4,294,967,296 different IP addresses. The IP address is composed of four groups of decimal digits, noted from 0 to 255, and separated by a dot (e.g. 86.212.113.159). It is the most widely used protocol in the world. It is used for both local IP addresses and public IP addresses.

To identify each other, the computers that make up the Internet network essentially use a series of numbers, each number (IP address) corresponding to a separate machine. The Internet Corporation for Assigned Names and Numbers (ICANN) coordinates these unique identifiers internationally and brings together, in a non-profit partnership, people from around the world who work to maintain the security, stability and interoperability of the Internet.

Often, in order to connect to a computer server, the user does not give his IP address, but his **domain name**. A domain is a set of computers connected to the Internet with a common characteristic. The domain name system is hierarchical, allowing the definition of sub-domains whose codes (levels) are separated by a dot. For example, the domain inp.cnrs.fr designates the CNRS

Institute of Physics in France. The rightmost part, such as "com", "net", "org" and "fr", is called the top-level domain. The domain name is then resolved to an IP address by the user's computer using the Domain Name System (DNS). It is possible to initiate a connection only once the address is obtained.

As the structure of the IPv4 address no longer made it possible to respond to all address requests, it was necessary to develop a new structure called IPv6, with 128 bits. This makes it possible to have over 256 billion billion billion billion billion different IP addresses!

2.4.6. *Management and use of the Internet*

The growing importance of the Internet has led to its very precise organization. The three main regulatory bodies are as follows:

– the Internet Society (ISOC) is dedicated to promoting and coordinating the development of computer networks worldwide. It is the most influential, moral and technical authority in the world of the Internet[2];

– the Internet Activity Board (IAB) provides guidance in coordinating much of the research and development related to TCP/IP protocols;

– the Internet Engineering Task Force (IETF) is an international open community of about 100 working groups that develop new Internet standards.

The growth of the Internet has been extraordinary, with 10,000 computers connected in 1987, 2.5 million in 1994, 17 million in 1997, 400 million in 2000 and 3.5 billion in 2017[3]. This development concerns the entire planet, as shown in Figure 2.14.

For France, in 2017 the ARCEP (*Autorité de Régulation des Communications Electroniques et des Postes*) announced 25 million people connected to high (ADSL)- or very high (fiber optic)-speed Internet, and about 70 million SIM cards providing access to the Internet.

---

2 The Internet Society regularly published its "Global Internet Reports", which are available at https://future.internetsociety.org/.

3 Source: Internet Society.

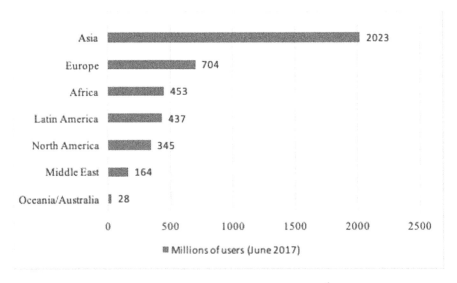

Figure 2.14. *Extension of the Internet[4]*

2.4.7. *Evolving technologies*

E-mail and file transfer are the oldest applications on the Internet. But the service that made the Internet popular with the general public is the World Wide Web, which began to spread in 1993 (more details on this are given in section 2.5.1). The rapid increase in the capabilities of computers meant that they were capable of encoding and processing sound or voice, as well as still images or video.

But interactive multimedia applications, such as videoconferencing, need efficient group (multi-user) transmission on the one hand, and performance guarantees on the other hand. Since the Internet is a network that provides a routing service without any guarantee of performance (Best Effort Principle), it was necessary to develop control mechanisms that allowed multimedia applications to adapt their behavior according to the conditions of the network.

The evolution of the Internet is taking place in parallel with an explosion of new applications, which seek to make the best use of the services available at any given moment. Examples include games distributed over the

---

4 Source: http://www.internetworldstats.com/stats.htm.

Internet (in which several thousand players around the world can compete on a battlefield or in a board game), or collaboration tools (distance learning, collaboration of doctors around scanner/X-ray images visible and writable by all). More generally, we can expect the Internet to represent a revolution that is at least comparable to the telephone revolution that began in the last century.

2.4.8. *What future?*

We are seeing that computer networks, especially the Internet, are having an ever-increasing impact on our daily lives. For better or for worse? In 2017, the Internet Society released a report entitled "Paths to our Digital Future"[5].

This report analyzes the key driving forces that will have a profound impact on the future of the Internet in the near future:

– the **convergence of the Internet and physical worlds** with the deployment of the Internet of Things (IoT). When everything that can be connected is connected, entire economies and societies will be transformed. However, acute security threats and device vulnerabilities, as well as incompatible standards and lack of interoperable systems could undermine the promise of technology;

– the **advent of artificial intelligence** (AI) promises new opportunities, ranging from new services and scientific breakthroughs to the increase of human intelligence and its convergence with the digital world. Ethical considerations must be prioritized in terms of the design and deployment of AI technologies;

– the most pressing danger for the future of the Internet is the **growing scope of cyber threats**. As new technologies such as AI and IoT increase our dependency on the network, the severity of security challenges and vulnerabilities increase in parallel;

– these technological transformations will disrupt **economic structures** and force companies to think and act like technology companies as billions of devices and sensors connect to the network;

---

5 Available at: https://future.internetsociety.org/2017/wp-content/uploads/sites/3/2017/09/2017-Internet-Society-Global-Internet-Report-Paths-to-Our-Digital-Future.pdf.

– as the Internet grows and extends to more sectors of our economy and society, **governments** will be faced with a host of new and complex issues that will challenge all aspects of their decision-making. Their responses to these challenges will influence not only freedoms, rights and the economy but also the Internet itself.

The report analyzes three areas of impact:

– as the Internet continues to transform all sectors of the global economy, the **digital divides** of the future are not only about access to the Internet but also about the gap between the economic opportunities available to some and not to others. These new divides will create disparities not only between countries but also within countries;

– the future of the Internet is closely linked to people's ability to see it as a means of improving society and promoting **individual rights** and **freedoms**. This trust needs to be confirmed and strengthened;

– the march towards greater connectivity will continue to drive new changes in **media** and **society**. While democratizing access to information, the whirlwind of information and misinformation that exists online raises real concerns about the long-term effects of new trends such as fake news. Unfettered online extremism and behavior that breaks social conventions will erode social cohesion, trust in the Internet and even political stability.

2.5. Applications

The above tells the story that led to the standardization of communications between computers of all sizes. But networks have changed profoundly: the volume of data traffic, the very rapid increase in the number of sites, broadband (20 Mbit/s at home), transporting multimedia data on the same medium (telephone, television, games, information, etc.), wireless mobile access, etc.

Here are some major areas of application, of which we will see more specific examples in Chapter 6.

2.5.1. *The World Wide Web*

The Web was invented in 1989 at CERN (European Organization for Nuclear Research), based in Geneva, by a British physicist, Tim Berners-Lee[6]. Originally, the project, called the World Wide Web or W3, was designed and developed with his colleague Robert Cailliau so that scientists working in universities and institutes around the world could exchange information instantaneously. On April 30, 1993, CERN put the World Wide Web software in the public domain. Tim Berners-Lee left CERN to go to the Massachusetts Institute of Technology (MIT) in 1994, where he founded the World Wide Web Consortium (W3C), an international community dedicated to the development of open web standards.

We all use the Web, without necessarily knowing it. A website is nothing more or less than a collection of files stored on a **web server**. **Web browsers** are applications that retrieve the content of pages, located on web servers, to send them to another computer, the latter being called a **web client**.

The Web is based on three main ideas: hypertext navigation, multimedia support and integration of pre-existing services (e-mail, file transfer, etc.). When writing a document (called a page) on the Web, certain words can be identified as access keys and a pointer to other documents can be associated with them. These other documents can be hosted on computers on the other side of the world.

In October 1990, Tim Berners-Lee described the three technologies that remain the foundation of today's Web:

– **HTML** (HyperText Markup Language): this language, standardized by the W3C, enables formatting documents for the Web;

– **URI** (Uniform Resource Identifier): a kind of address that is unique and used to identify each resource on the Web. It is also commonly referred to as a URL;

– **HTTP** (HyperText Transfer Protocol): standardized by the IETF, this network protocol allows the recovery of linked resources across the Web.

---

6 A British engineer born in 1955, he invented the World Wide Web, its protocols and languages (HTTP, HTML), and the URLs used to uniquely identify sites. Creator of the W3C, the organization that regulates the Web, he is also at the origin of the semantic web, which can be interpreted by machines thanks to semantic technologies.

2.5.1.1. *HTML*

HTML was invented to allow writing hypertextual documents, also called web pages, linking the different resources of the Internet with hyperlinks. It is a so-called markup language (or structuring language), whose role is to formalize the writing of a document with formatting tags. The tags make it possible to indicate the way in which the document should be presented and the links it establishes with other documents.

Here is an example of an HTML file, with a title and a body of two paragraphs, one of which contains a hyperlink:

```
<!DOCTYPE html>
<html>
 <head.
 <title>Example HTML file</title>
 </head>
 <body
 A sentence with a <a href="target.html">hyperlink</a>.
 <p>
    A paragraph where there is no hyperlink.
 </p>
 </body>
</html>
```

Since HTML does not attach to the final rendering of the document, the same HTML document can be viewed using a wide variety of hardware (computer, tablet, smartphone, etc.), which must have the appropriate software (web browser, for example) to provide the final rendering.

A web browser is a software program designed to view and display especially HTML pages. Technically, it is at least an HTTP client. Let us mention a few web browsers: Netscape (1994), Internet Explorer (1995), Mozilla (1998) and Firefox (2005), Safari (2003), etc.

The standards for this language have evolved (successive versions) to take into account the new possibilities offered by Internet navigation.

2.5.1.2. *HTTP*

HTTP (Hypertext Transfer Protocol) is a communication protocol developed for the World Wide Web. It was designed for the transfer of hypermedia documents such as HTML. It follows the classic "client–server" model, with a client that opens a connection to send a request, then waits until a response is received. HTTPS (with an S for *secured*) is the secure HTTP variant.

The best known HTTP clients are web browsers. The user's computer uses the browser to send a request to a web server. This request asks for a document (e.g. an HTML page, an image, a file). The server looks for the information to finally send the response.

Figure 2.15. *HTTP request*

2.5.1.3. *URL addresses*

Website addresses, also called URL (Uniform Resource Locator) addresses, look more or less like this: http://www.example.com. Every document, image or web page has a URL address, which is often used to link to it.

A URL consists of at least the following parts:

– the name of the protocol, that is, the language used to communicate on the network. The most widely used protocol is the HTTP protocol that we have just talked about, but many other protocols are useful (FTP, News, Mailto, etc.);

– the name of the server: this is the domain name of the computer hosting the requested resource;

– the access path to the resource: this last part allows the server to know the location of the resource, that is, in general, the directory and the name of the requested file.

For example, "http://www.xxxx.fr/" identifies company server xxxx and leads to the site's home page. The URL "http://www.xxxx.fr/presentation. html" identifies the company's presentation page.

We use less and less directly URLs due to our intensive use of search engines such as Google or Yahoo.

2.5.2. *Cloud computing*

The electrical equipment in our homes uses energy that comes from "somewhere". We do not have to worry about the source of this energy, which is diversified and can change depending on the period, since these sources (nuclear power plants, hydroelectric power plants, etc.) are interconnected by networks that guarantee that we are always supplied.

Cloud computing uses the metaphor of clouds to symbolize the dematerialization of computing. It involves moving IT services to remote servers, managed by suppliers and accessible via the Internet, and thus having access to virtually infinite services and resources (storage, computing).

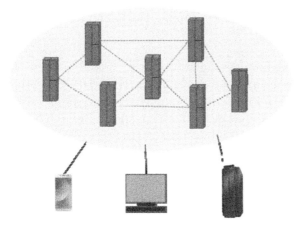

Figure 2.16. *Cloud computing*

Cloud computing is of interest to individuals (e.g. to store photos and videos), small businesses (which thus have access to resources they could not afford) and large companies alike.

There are three types of cloud computing:

– IaaS (Infrastructure as a Service): the operating system and applications are installed by the client on servers to which he connects to work as if it were his own computer. Physical resources are shared by several virtual machines;

– PaaS (Platform as a Service): the service provider manages the operating system and associated tools on its platform. The client develops, installs and uses his own applications;

– SaaS (Software as a Service): applications are provided as turnkey services to which users connect via dedicated software or a web browser.

The client cannot locate the physical sites that host these services, and these sites are subject to change. The advantages are numerous: cost reduction by shifting IT to the provider, ease of use from any location thanks to the Internet, quality of service, flexibility to manage peak loads, etc. Application and data security is, of course, a critical aspect and it is essential to address it. Some companies avoid this solution for storing and processing highly sensitive data.

The cloud computing market is huge, and there are many solution providers: major computer manufacturers (IBM, HP, etc.), Amazon, Google, Microsoft, OVH in France to name only the most significant. According to Synergy Group, the turnover of cloud computing suppliers reached 180 billion dollars for the period October 2016–September 2017 with an overall growth of 24%.

2.5.3. *The Internet of Things*

While the Internet was designed for humans to communicate and access information, the idea is that objects can exchange information and humans can acquire information through objects.

Imagine a world where all objects are able to exchange information and communicate with each other, as well as to communicate and interact with their users through the Internet and other less well-known but equally effective communication networks. This is the world of the Internet of Things.

A connected object has the ability to capture data and send it, via the Internet or other technologies, for analysis and use. These billions of connected objects will create an exponential volume of data that will need to be stored, analyzed, secured and restored for various uses.

Analysts predict more than 50 billion connected objects in a few years. This connected and intelligent world is expected to explode the volume of data from 8 zettabytes (8 trillion billion) in 2015 to 180 zettabytes in 2025, 95% of which will be unstructured data (text data, JPEG images, MP3 audio files, etc.); a volume that is expected to be 92% processed in the Cloud (Huawei's prospective report).

2.5.3.1. *Main technologies*

In terms of technologies, standardized wireless access (such as Wi-Fi and Bluetooth) currently dominates due to the strong development of consumer applications (connected home, sports/wellness, electronic gadgets) and of course its low cost. New technologies and protocols have been and are still being developed to take into account the constraints and specificities of the many areas of IoT use (energy consumption, for example). We mention below the most used ones.

NFC (Near-Field Communication) is a technology that allows data to be exchanged at a distance of less than 10 cm between two devices equipped with this device. NFC is integrated in most of our mobile terminals in the form of a chip, as well as on certain transport, payment or access control cards for restricted access premises. The reader can simply operate the unlock or be connected to a network to transmit the information corresponding to your entry. In the latter case, you enter the IoT domain.

RFID (Radio Frequency Identification) is a technology that enables memorizing and retrieving data remotely using radio tags (RFID tags) that can be stuck or embedded in objects and even implanted in living organisms (animals, human body). The reading of passive chips can extend up to 200 meters. This technology is widely used in business.

Low-Energy Bluetooth (also known by the acronym BLE and Bluetooth Smart) is replacing NFC and is mainly intended for connected objects where the need for throughput is low and battery life is crucial, as well as nomadic equipment such as smartphones, tablets, watches, etc. The range can be counted in a few dozen meters.

Short-range radio protocols (ZigBee, Z-Wave) are intended for the creation of private local area networks (for home automation, for example). They are energy efficient and offer high data rates.

Low-speed radio protocols (Sigfox, LoRa) are particularly suitable for energy-efficient equipment that emits only periodically, such as sensors.

LTE-A, or LTE Advanced, is a fourth-generation cell phone network standard. It gives the IoT much more performance, and its most important applications concern vehicles and other terminals in motion.

2.5.3.2. Fields of use

The value added by the Internet of Things is in the new uses it will bring. Let us retain the most important ones; we will detail some of them in Chapter 6.

The sector is carried by the smart home: connected security devices (wireless surveillance cameras, alarms, etc.) and those dedicated to the automation of the home (thermostats, locks, intercoms), not forgetting the large connected household appliances (refrigerators, washing machines, etc.) and robots. The "smart city" is another important area: road traffic, transportation, waste collection, various mapping (noise, energy, etc.).

Wearable technologies are developing: connected watches and glasses, smart clothing, etc. They are also found in the monitoring of our health (connected scales, monitoring of patients with chronic diseases), in leisure and sports and in many toys.

Other areas include: environmental monitoring (earthquake prediction, fire detection, air quality, etc.), industry (measurement, prognosis and prediction of breakdowns), logistics (automated warehouses), vehicles that require more autonomy and robots in various environments.

Here is now a very common example: contactless means of payment using a bank card, a cell phone or a bracelet which communicates with payment terminals using the NFC communication protocol already mentioned; we therefore avoid inserting the bank card and entering a confidential code. This protocol allows data to be exchanged at a very short distance (a few centimeters). A chip and an antenna are integrated into your bank card, your cell phone, etc. Via a smartphone, the applications dedicated to NFC payment can also include a certain number of additional and very useful functions such as the automatic taking into account of loyalty cards in stores. But do we know all the features and what is done with the information collected?

2.5.3.3. *Towards the interoperability of objects*

Each object has an often simple function. But if several objects can be made to collaborate, to make them interoperable, their capabilities will be considerably increased. This is, for example, the ability of industrial robots to communicate directly with each other or the ability of different connected objects involved in flow management (factory, hospital, etc.).

A major obstacle: the connectivity of objects is dominated by proprietary technologies, often developed without technical or legal standardization.

2.5.3.4. *Confidentiality and security*

Whether in the medical field (patient tracking devices), the automotive industry (connected cars), agriculture (precision farming) or home automation, devices that take advantage of the Internet of Things generate an unprecedented amount of data. These data are often confidential and personal. Are they really protected?

When you turn on your connected speaker, what is said in the room is recorded somewhere. Your question, "What will the weather be like tomorrow?" will be analyzed by the computer system to understand it and provide you with the answer. But your conversation will also be recorded if you are not careful. Who can use this information and for what purpose?

Moreover, connected objects represent a risk in terms of cybersecurity. These devices are designed to be as simple as possible, in order to limit their cost and facilitate their use. However, this simplicity also makes them more vulnerable than other electronic devices such as smartphones.

Gartner Inc., a US-based advanced technology consulting and research firm, announced that global spending on Internet of Things security was expected to reach $1.5 billion in 2018.

2.5.4. *Ubiquitous computing and spontaneous networks*

2.5.4.1. *Ubiquitous computing*

The multiplication of connected objects leads to an important aspect of the development of computing. We have gone from "mainframe computers" in the hands of specialists (computer scientists) to personal computers that can be used simply by anyone thanks to highly efficient graphical interfaces. We are entering a third era, one in which computers are disappearing, leaving us in a hyper-connected world in which the computer is invisible.

This vision of ubiquitous computing (the term is derived from the Latin *ubique* meaning "everywhere"), which is constantly available, was first formulated in 1988 by Mark Weiser of the Xerox Palo Alto Research Center. It is also referred to as ambient intelligence and pervasive computing.

In Mark Weiser's idea, computer tools are embedded in everyday objects. The objects are used both at work and at home. According to him, "the deepest technologies are those that have become invisible. Those which, knotted together, form the fabric of our daily life to the point of becoming inseparable from it".

Today's IT systems are decentralized, diverse, highly connected, easy to use and often invisible. A whole range of discrete devices communicate discreetly through a fabric of heterogeneous networks.

2.5.4.2. *Spontaneous and autonomous networks*

Spontaneous and autonomous networks, also called *ad hoc* networks, have an important place in this development. *Ad hoc* networks (Latin for "who goes where he must go", i.e. "formed for a specific purpose", such as an *ad hoc* commission formed to solve a particular problem) are wireless networks capable of organizing themselves without a predefined infrastructure.

The first research on "*ad hoc* multi-hop" networks dates back to the 1960s and was carried out by DARPA, as the military was very interested in this approach for the battlefield.

Ad hoc networks, in their most common mobile configuration, are known as MANET (for Mobile Ad hoc NETworks). MANET is also the name of an IETF working group, created in 1998–1999, tasked with standardizing IP-based routing protocols for wireless *ad hoc* networks.

A MANET network is characterized by:

– the lack of a centralized infrastructure. Nodes have one or more wireless interfaces and have routing features that allow a packet to reach its destination from node to node without a designated router;

– a dynamic topology. The mobile units of the network add, disappear and move in a free and arbitrary way. Therefore, the topology of the network can change, at unpredictable moments, in a fast and random way;

– the heterogeneity of the nodes;

– an energy constraint. Mobile equipment generally has limited batteries. Knowing that part of the energy is already consumed by the routing functionality, the services and applications supported by each node are limited;

– limited bandwidth;

– vulnerability. The possibilities of insertion in the network are greater, the detection of an intrusion or a denial of service more delicate and the absence of centralization poses a problem of information feedback of intrusion detection;

– the system can operate in isolation or interface to fixed networks through gateways.

These technologies are particularly used in sensor networks. The sensor is a device that transforms the state of an observed physical and/or logical quantity into a usable quantity. Wireless sensor networks are considered a special type of *ad hoc* networks where fixed communication infrastructure and centralized administration are absent and nodes play the role of both hosts and routers.

This type of network consists of a set of micro-sensors scattered across a geographical area called the catchment field, which defines the terrain of interest for the phenomenon being captured. The deployed micro-sensors are capable of continuously monitoring a wide variety of ambient conditions.

Sensor networks respond to the emergence of an increased need for diffuse and automatic observation and monitoring of complex physical and biological phenomena in various fields: industrial (quality control of a manufacturing chain), environmental (monitoring of pollutants, seismic risk, etc.), security (risk of failure of large-scale equipment such as a dam), etc.

2.6. Networks and security

2.6.1. *Vulnerabilities*

Networks are fuelling ever-increasing cybercrime, not to mention their use for malicious political purposes, which has been in the news since 2017.

In May 2017, hackers attacked thousands of governments and businesses around the world with malware, blocking the use of computers and demanding ransom. Considering the largest ransomware cyber attack in history to date, WannaCry infected more than 300,000 computers across more than 150 countries in a matter of hours.

The US-based credit company Equifax was the target of a massive hacking attack in 2017. The information of more than 140 million Americans and more than 200,000 consumer credit card numbers were accessed by hackers. This attack exploited a vulnerability in one of the company's applications, allowing access to certain secret files.

The main objectives of computer attacks are:

– to get access to your computer or system;

– to steal information, including personal data and bank data;

– to disrupt the proper functioning of the service;

– to use the system as a rebound for an attack.

There are several types of malware:

– **viruses** are software that can be installed on a computer without the knowledge of its legitimate user;

– reticular viruses (**botnet**) are spread on millions of computers connected to the Internet;

– a **Trojan horse** is a software program that presents itself in an honest light and, once installed on a computer, performs hidden actions on it;

– a **backdoor** is hidden communication software, installed, for example, by a virus or a Trojan horse, which gives an external attacker access to the victim computer through the network;

– **spyware** collects, without the knowledge of the legitimate user, information and communicates it to an external agent;

– unsolicited electronic mail (**spam**) consists of massive electronic communications, in particular e-mails, without solicitation of the recipients, for advertising or dishonest purposes. It is a scourge, and it is estimated that 70% of the e-mail circulating around the world is just spam;

– **phishing** is a fraudulent technique used by hackers to retrieve information (usually banking information) from Internet users. This technique consists of deceiving Internet users by means of an e-mail that appears to come from a trusted company, such as a bank or a trading company.

A denial of service attack is a type of attack designed to make an organization's services or resources (usually servers) unavailable for an indefinite period of time. There are two types: denial of service by saturation and denial of service by exploiting vulnerabilities.

It is essential to put in place measures to secure networks to ensure:

– **confidentiality**, which aims to ensure that only authorized persons have access to the resources and information to which they are entitled;

– **authenticity**, which makes it possible to verify the identity of the actors of communication;

– **integrity**, which aims to ensure that resources and information are not corrupted, altered or destroyed;

– **availability**, which is intended to ensure that the system is ready to use and that services are accessible.

2.6.2. *The protection of a network*

We have the ability to protect our personal network or that of our organization against certain attacks from outside. Several complementary methods are available. We can limit communication and visibility from the outside. The most commonly used method is the implementation of a firewall that forces the passage through a single point of control (inbound and outbound: Who? For what?). Its main task is to control traffic between different trusted zones by filtering the data flows that pass through them.

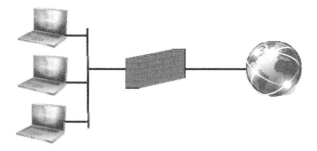

Figure 2.17. *Firewall diagram*

2.6.3. *Message encryption*

Encryption is a process of cryptography through which we wish to make the understanding of a document impossible for anyone who does not have the decryption key. Cryptography is very old and children, even today, can still have fun encrypting messages, with simple codes, so that their parents do not understand the meaning!

There are two main families of encryption: symmetric and asymmetric encryption. Symmetric encryption allows us to encrypt and decrypt content with the same key, known as the secret key. Symmetric encryption is particularly fast, but requires the sender and receiver to agree on a common secret key or to transmit it via another channel.

Asymmetric encryption assumes that the (future) recipient has a pair of keys (private key, public key) and has ensured that potential senders have access to its public key. In this case, the sender uses the recipient's public key to encrypt the message while the recipient uses his private key to decrypt it.

2.6.4. *Checking its security*

It is essential for everyone to ensure the security of their IT environment, even if it is just a personal computer. Here are a few simple rules:

– backup your data; do not keep the backups in the same place, check that they are working;

– update the anti-virus;

– check the security of access (wired or Wi-Fi) to its environment;

– manage spam and phishing attempts properly (vigilance, system destruction, reporting to the operator and the organizations in charge of fighting cybercrime).

3

Software

3.1. Introduction

In the preface to this book, we mentioned the triangle representing the pillars of information technology. Chapters 1 and 2 dealt with two of these pillars: computer hardware, on the one hand, and means of communication, on the other hand. This is the third pillar, probably the most important, because the concepts of algorithm and software are at the heart of computing.

A computer system is a set of hardware or software components, put together to collaborate in the execution of an application.

A computer system can be described as a stack of layers, each one resting on the underlying layer and providing new and more elaborate functions. Adapted interfaces allow these layers to communicate with each other.

Figure 3.1 is a simplified representation of a computer system.

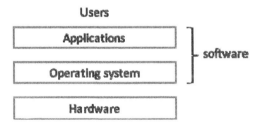

Figure 3.1. *Computer system*

Hardware is composed of processors, memories, disks and peripheral units (screen, mouse, printer, etc.). The operation of the hardware is based on instructions composed of only 0 and 1, and is said to have the lowest layer of abstraction at the hardware level.

The operating system (the core and utilities that provide basic services to the user) is the central element of the system. This layer will support the communication between applications and hardware, and ensure the execution of the instructions it has received from the application. Special languages will be used to build the operating system programs.

The application is what the user manipulates. The user does not, in general, need to know the operating system, let alone the hardware layer. The user sees the application as a virtual machine which will manage the communications with the underlying layer, the operating system. This virtual machine will also be able to operate thanks to programs built with languages.

We will see that some system architectures, for example distributed systems, require additional layers that are often called middleware.

Software is therefore a very large set of computer programs, each with specific characteristics and functions. The way of programming will be very different if it is a question of writing a web page, the driver of a peripheral device, the tasks of an industrial robot or the user interface of a smartphone: programming environment, language(s), security constraints, etc.

This chapter aims to describe this diversity of programming languages and software at one level or another of this layered structure, as well as the main aspects of software development. It will end with a presentation of the ways in which software is protected and distributed.

3.2. From algorithm to computer program

We discussed algorithms in Chapter 1, and remember that an algorithm is simply a way of describing, in great detail, how to do something "mechanically". Algorithms can be written without any link to computer science, as shown with the example of the recipe!

The algorithm must accurately translate what you want to do, the "intent". And there are always several ways to do this translation, so several ways to build an algorithm to solve a well-defined problem. However, there is almost always a better way, according to various criteria (speed, required memory space, etc.).

We have already described an algorithm to compute the PGCD of two numbers. We now want to calculate the factorial F of a natural number N. It is the product of strictly positive integers less than or equal to N, and it is 1 if N = 0. For example, the factorial of 5 is 1 x 2 x 3 x 4 x 5 = 120. The direct method is based on the finding that the factorial of N is equal to N multiplied by the factorial of (N − 1). The algorithm can then be described as follows (Figure 3.2):

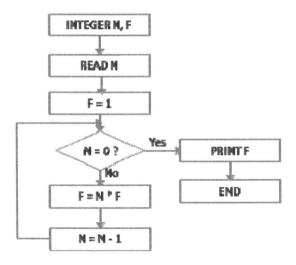

Figure 3.2. *Flowchart for computing factorial N*

This algorithm does not check that the number N is not negative. If, by some misfortune, I get a negative N read even though the statement says that N is positive or zero, the algorithm will never end; there will be what is called a bug. Adding this test in the algorithm would therefore not be useless.

This algorithm can be expressed in a programming language taking into account the specific syntax of this language and the four ingredients: variables, instructions that execute sequentially, tests, and loops.

Variables can be seen as boxes, for example memory areas, in which values can be put. Each variable, here F and N, has a value at a given time. These variables can be complex, and we can find (beyond numerical values and character strings) lists, tables, graphs and containers corresponding to images, sounds, etc.

An **instruction** or sequence of instructions transforms a state, that is, the value of variables. In our example, the value of variables N and F is modified by instructions.

In the sequences, we can introduce branches from **tests** (if the condition is true then I do this, if not I do that) and **loops** (repeat this as many times as necessary). In our case, there is a test (Is N equal to zero?) and a loop, which is the repetition of three instructions. We could simplify this writing with a loop instruction like:

```
FOR N RANGING FROM N TO 1, CALCULATE F=N*F
```

The algorithm is thus the abstract skeleton of the computer program, independent of the particular coding mode, which will allow its effective implementation within a computer system.

3.2.1. *Programs and subprograms*

The processing required from a computer is generally complex, and it is impossible to describe it with a single global algorithm. The computer program that translates it can contain hundreds of thousands or even millions of lines. We will break down the problem into less complex subproblems that will facilitate the structuring and writing of the program.

A subprogram is a block of instructions performing a certain processing. It has a name and is executed when it is called upon. This processing involves data; the value of which may change from one call of the subprogram to another. The data transmitted to the subprogram by the main program are the parameters of the subprogram.

There are two types of subprograms:

– a **procedure** is a subprogram that does not return a result; its role is to perform side effects, that is, to have an action on objects or variables that exist outside the procedure;

– a **function** is a subprogram that will return a result to the main program, just like a mathematical function does.

Subprograms offer the means to create relatively independent programming modules that can be developed, checked separately, and reused as many times as desired. You can also use subprograms written by colleagues or available in program libraries; there are many of them, often adapted to particular contexts.

3.2.2. *Programming languages*

The algorithm describes precisely what I want to do. My goal is that this description becomes an operational realization: a database of my music records (categories, musicians, location on my shelves, etc.), a web page describing my family tree, the calculation of the factorial of a positive or null integer. I need to translate this algorithm by writing a computer program in a language that I know, or that I could learn, and that could eventually become an executable program by the computer system I will have access to.

The problem is that the computer's processor only knows how to process sequences of 0 and 1, so it has to be told in binary code which operations it has to execute, operations being globally of four types:

– arithmetic operations;

– logical operations;

– read and write operations in memory;

– control operations (unconditional or conditional connections).

If I do not "speak" **machine language**, the only one that the processor understands, I will need an automatic translation system between my **programming language** and the language the computer understands. This is the role of particular programs called **compilers** or **interpreters**.

A programming language is a conventional notation for formulating algorithms and producing computer programs that apply them. In a similar way to the English language, a programming language is composed of an alphabet, a vocabulary, grammar rules and meanings. All languages must follow a precise syntax; when learning a language, we must first learn the syntax.

Depending on the programming language's level of abstraction, a language can be said to be "low level", consisting of elementary instructions close to the machine (assembler, for example), or "high level", consisting of more abstract instructions that can be translated into a certain number of elementary instructions (Fortran, Pascal, C++, Lisp, etc.).

Computer languages are to be considered at several levels of abstraction, from the lowest, closest to the electronic components, to the highest, closest to the user, more independent of the hardware.

Hundreds, even thousands of languages have been defined and implemented. There are many reasons for this:

– evolution of the discipline: progress in description formalisms, progress in compilation techniques, new currents in methodology (structured programming, modular programming, object-oriented programming, etc.);

– evolution of computer architecture;

– the variety of problems to be solved: very complex data structures, human–machine interfaces, embedded systems, highly secure applications, etc.

A few hundred languages are probably still in use, and a few dozen are used to a large extent.

The success of a language depends on several factors, including

– the power of expression: any language can express everything, but more or less easily;

– ease of use;

– the ease of implementation on various machines;

– the quality of the implementation: good performance, user-friendliness of the related tools;

– the extent of the existing community around the language.

Figure 3.3 presents a hierarchical approach to the main programming languages, referring to "basic" rather than "low-level" software because it is on them that the whole computer system and application software is based, taking into account the interfaces, of which the compilers are the main element.

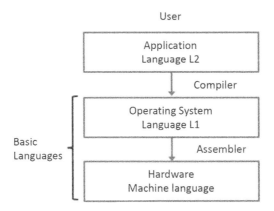

Figure 3.3. *Hierarchy of programming languages*

3.3. Basic languages and operating systems

3.3.1. *Basic languages*

Basic or "low-level" languages are used to control the machine's operation. A distinction is made between machine language and the languages associated with the development of the operating system.

A processor, by design of its architecture, knows only a reduced number of instructions, called its instruction set, which allows it to execute arithmetic and logical operations, to make data movements between memory and registers, connections, etc.

Since it only includes instructions coded in binary (0 and 1), a program intended for it will have to be written in the machine language specific to its architecture. The "words" of a machine language are instructions, each of which triggers an action on the part of the processor. These words are composed of 0 and 1, for example 10110000 01100001.

How do we directly program the instructions available on a processor? Writing a program using machine language is a challenge and assembly languages have been created to simplify this work. An assembly language provides a symbolic representation of a machine language. An instruction in this language corresponds to an instruction in the machine language.

In the assembly language, an instruction consists of the mnemonic code of the type of operation and the symbolic representations of the operands.

For example, the instruction:

```
MOV DESTINATION, ORIGIN
```

will copy the data from the ORIGIN address into the contents of the DESTINATION address.

A special program, called the **assembler**, will translate the program written in assembler language (**source code**) into machine language (**object code**). There can be several assembly languages for the same processor, each with its own syntax (e.g. Intel, AT&T or Microsoft syntax for the x86 processor) and as many assemblers as assembly languages. The result, from the point of view of the machine program, is of course the same.

In short, the processor only understands instructions written in its machine language; these instructions can be written in an assembly language and then translated by an assembler.

3.3.2. *Operating system functions*

The assembly language is the basic language used to write the programs that constitute the Operating System (OS), which has two essential roles:

– offer users a simplified interface to allow them to get rid of the complexity of the physical machine, thus offering a more absent-minded version (virtual machine) of the underlying physical machine;

– optimally manage the hardware and software resources needed to launch and monitor the execution of local or remote applications.

It is composed of two main parts:

– the kernel that is loaded at boot time and performs basic functions such as program execution, hardware (memory, processor, peripherals, etc.) and network protocol (TCP/IP, etc.) management, user management, etc.;

– a set of utility programs offering higher-level services: editors, browser, messaging service, etc.

Without going into detail, the main functions of the OS can be summarized as follows:

– **processors**: processors must be used as efficiently as possible while sharing their time between the different applications that use them. Each program is executed during a specific time period, and then the OS switches to running another program;

– **memory**: the OS is in charge of managing the memory space (reservation, release after use) requested by each application and, if necessary, by each user. Memory management is important because poor management will have an impact on overall performance;

– **peripheral units**: the OS enables unifying and controlling program access to hardware resources (keyboard, printer, hard disk, etc.) via drivers;

– **files**: the OS manages reading and writing in the file system and file access rights for users and applications;

– **networks**: the OS contains the necessary programs for information exchange in different protocols from levels 1 to 4 (the OSI model we have already described);

– **access control**: the OS must ensure that resources are used only by programs and users with appropriate rights;

– **user interfaces**: the OS ensures communication with the user (mouse, screen with graphical user interface, for example) and with the applications.

Let us continue this layered approach with Figure 3.4, which illustrates the OS's role.

The operating system somehow masks the complexity of the lower level, the hardware. It thus presents a kind of virtual machine to its user. And this will become increasingly important with the growing complexity of computer systems, especially the space taken up by distributed systems.

Figure 3.4. *Role of the operating system. For a color version of this figure, see www.iste.co.uk/delhaye/computing.zip*

3.3.3. *A bit of history*

Operating systems have, of course, evolved considerably over time.

3.3.3.1. *Monoprogramming*

The early OSs were very simple: the program was read (usually on punched cards), the computer would run the program, print the results, and then move on to the next program. The sequence of jobs was done by a program called a monitor, or batch processing system, and this was the first form of an operating system. This was called monoprogramming (managing only one program at a time), which had, among other faults, a misuse of the CPU: while a card was being read or a line printed, the CPU would wait, because computers of the time could only do one thing at a time.

3.3.3.2. *Multiprogramming*

Innovations in the management of peripheral units and an increase in memory size have enabled a new execution scheme, multiprogramming, which consists of making several programs coexist simultaneously in memory, and in taking advantage of the dead times of a program (e.g. input–output operations) to "advance" the other programs. In early multiprogramming systems, the memory was divided into fixed-sized areas in which user programs were loaded (this was the case in the MFT version of IBM's OS/360). Later, the limits of these zones, in variable number, were dynamically adjustable (the MFT version was replaced by MVT,

Multiprogramming with a Variable number of Tasks), which allowed a better use of the memory.

3.3.3.3. Time-sharing

Users do not yet have the ability to interact with the program they are asking the machine to run. Time-sharing systems have transformed the way computers are managed. The principle of time-sharing is simple: it is about taking advantage of the speed differences between a computer, then clocked at the microsecond, and a human whose interaction time including reflection and command keystrokes is several seconds. Once a user's request has been processed, the computer moves on to the next user's request, then to the next user and so on. Virtually all current systems incorporate the concept of time-sharing.

3.3.3.4. Virtual memory

One can imagine that the operating system becomes more complex, especially since it is necessary to manage the memory which is limited in size and is shared between several users. We will therefore discover the so-called virtual memory technology that allows a computer to compensate for the lack of physical memory by transferring data pages from the central memory to an external storage (disk, for example). When the OS needs certain pages to run the program, it frees up some space in the main memory by transferring pages that are not needed at that moment so that it can load the necessary parts of the running program. This process is called **paging**.

3.3.3.5. Real time

Some operating systems must meet strong constraints; this is the case for real-time systems. These are systems whose correction depends not only on the values of the results produced but also on the time frame in which the results are produced. The system must respond to external *stimuli* within a specified delay. This is the case in the control of vehicles (including aircraft), robotics, industrial process control, etc.

3.3.3.6. Distributed systems

After multiprogramming systems, then time sharing or real time, the arrival of distributed systems has complicated the architecture of operating systems. A distributed system is a set of computers, independent, networked and cooperating to take advantage of the various physical resources (processors, memories, etc.) available. It is not easy to make this distributed system appear to a user as a single, coherent system. A layer of software (middleware) is interposed between the operating system and the elements of the distributed application. It is responsible for managing heterogeneity (programming languages, operating systems used, etc.) and will offer one or more communication services between the elements forming the application.

3.3.3.7. *Embedded systems*

Finally, the widespread use of embedded systems in almost all everyday devices has given rise to the development of systems adapted to specific devices and applications: mobile telephony (smartphones), sensor networks, automotive, avionics, etc. These systems are generally smaller and simpler than general-purpose systems.

3.3.3.8. *Some dates*

Let us take a look at a few dates that have marked the history of operating systems:

– 1962: General Electric began development of **GCOS** (General Comprehensive Operating System). As a mainframe-oriented system in the field of management, its history is linked to that of the manufacturers Honeywell, then Honeywell-Bull, and then Bull. This system, which has evolved considerably, is still used on some Bull platforms.

– 1965: MIT and Bell Laboratories launched the **Multics** (MULTiplexed Information and Computing Service) project, an ambitious time-sharing system. Taken over by Honeywell and then Bull, it equipped numerous computers (from Bull's IRIS range) in French university computing centers right through to the 1980s. The development of Unix used a significant proportion of Multics, simplifying it.

– 1965: launch of **OS/360**, the operating system developed by IBM for its System/360 series. Like other proprietary systems, it is no longer used.

– 1970: launch of **Unix**, which we will discuss in section 3.3.4.1.

– 1977: DEC created **VMS** (Virtual Memory System) for its VAX computers. It is no longer used today.

– 1981: IBM announced **DOS** (Disk Operating System) on the occasion of the launch of its IBM-PC. It was taken over by Microsoft with **MS-DOS**.

– 1984: **Mac OS** (now macOS), a graphical user interface operating system, was developed by Apple to equip its Macintosh personal computers. We will talk more about it in section 3.3.5.1.2.

– 1985: Microsoft launched **Windows**. We will come back to this in section 3.3.5.1.1.

– 1991: Linus Torvalds created **Linux**.

Over the years, operating systems that did not disappear experienced new versions, made necessary by technological developments (architectures, hardware, etc.). New OSs have appeared, in particular to meet the demand for mobile equipment and the explosion of the market for connected objects.

We have situated OSs between hardware and applications, so it makes sense to look at the broad categories of OSs based on hardware and application characteristics.

3.3.4. *Universal operating systems*

Today, there are two main classes of "universal systems": Unix-based OSs and Linux-based OSs.

3.3.4.1. *Unix*

UNIX occupies a central place in the history of IT. This OS is not aimed at the general public but at organizations, their servers and workstations.

The Unix system is a multi-user, multi-tasking operating system that was developed beginning in 1970 by Ken Thompson and Dennis Ritchie at AT&T's Bell Labs. First written in assembler language, it was then written in C language, which made it possible to modify it before compiling it and thus facilitated its porting to various processors.

In 1977, two branches of development were created: the branch commercialized by AT&T which was to become System V of UNIX System Labs (USL) and the BSD branch (Berkeley Software Distribution) distributed free of charge by the University of California.

Various versions of Unix were developed by major manufacturers, including:

– **AIX**, commercial Unix based on System V developed by IBM in 1990;

– **Sun OS**, later called Solaris, developed by Sun Microsystems (1982);

– **HP-UX**, commercial Unix based on System V, developed in 1986 by Hewlett Packard.

The large number of Unix variants, each with its own specificities, has allowed Unix systems to be used in many different environments. However, this diversity posed serious problems of communication between systems, which led manufacturers to turn to GNU/Linux.

3.3.4.2. Linux

In 1991, Linus Torvalds[1], a student at the University of Helsinki (Finland), started to develop a Unix kernel for his own use and published the source code on the Internet. Many developers joined this project and gradually turned it into a full operating system. This system took the name Linux, in reference to the name of its creator (Linux is the contraction of Linus and Unix).

Linux is therefore, from the outset, an operating system kernel that enables management of the execution of applications on any computer equipment. Today, the complete Linux system, including kernel and utilities, is freely available with its source code to anyone wishing to use, modify and redistribute it (GNU or General Public License; we will specify this notion of license in section 3.7.2).

In particular, thanks to its open-source model (freely available source code), Linux has made it possible to give rise to hundreds of Linux OSs or distributions, that is, complete operating systems based on this kernel. These distributions can be designed to play an OS role on a PC, a connected object, a server, etc. Among the most popular Linux distributions are Linux Mint, Linux Ubuntu, Red Hat, Debian, Suse Linux, Kali Linux and Arch Linux, each of which has its own specificities.

---

1 Linus Torvalds, born in 1969 in Helsinki, Finland, is one of the pioneers of a change in the way of thinking in the world of computing by proposing a non-commercial conception of its use, by developing and democratizing free software. Based in the United States, he continues to lead the Linux kernel development team.

Linux has conquered many consumer devices: music players, ISP boxes, personal assistants, GPS, phones, etc. The 500 most powerful supercomputers in the world are now also running on this system. It is still very much in the minority on personal computers (less than 2%) because its use requires good computer skills, even though the open-source community has produced a large number of software programs that can be used in many areas (office automation, multimedia, Internet, etc.).

In the end, Linux continues to evolve thanks to a very strong community of users around the world.

3.3.5. *Targeted operating systems*

3.3.5.1. *For personal computers*

3.3.5.1.1. Windows

More than 30 years ago, on November 20, 1985, Microsoft (founded in 1975 by Bill Gates and Paul Allen) introduced Windows 1.01. It was more of a GUI (Graphical User Interface) than an OS because it was based on the DOS system bought from IBM.

Successive versions of Windows, the most recent (as of 2019) being Windows 10 available since July 2015, have made it a very complete system whose popularity, due in part to the Microsoft Office product line (Word, Excel, etc.), has continued to grow. Windows now equips hundreds of millions of PCs (compatible with the range of personal computers derived from the IBM PC) and remains the undisputed leader in this market. According to the NetMarketShare site, Windows equips 88% of personal computers (end of 2018).

Microsoft has also developed Windows Server, which is an operating system in its own right, intended for use in companies. It allows you to administer large computer equipment, manage user accounts, group policies, messaging, etc.

3.3.5.1.2. macOS

Apple's first operating system, designed to equip its personal computers, came to fruition in 1984. In 1997, the name Mac OS (Macintosh Operating System) appeared. Mac OS is part of the Unix family of operating systems.

The first version of Mac OS X was released in 2001 and versions follow one another.

In 2016, Apple chose to rename OS X to macOS in order to harmonize the name with the other OSs of the brand (iOS, watchOS, tvOS). The most recent version (October 2019) is macOS Catalina (OS 10.15).

According to the same NetMarketShare site, by the end of 2018, Apple's OS would equip nearly 10% of personal computers.

Like Microsoft, Apple has developed a server version of macOS called macOS Server.

3.3.5.2. *Nomadic operating systems*

Smartphones and tablets have specific operating systems that must take into account the mobility of users, the limitations of mobile terminals in terms of computing power, memory capacity and energy autonomy. Systems have had to become lighter to adapt to these new constraints.

Nearly all manufacturers have started to develop an OS for their products. We can cite Symbian OS, which was used by Samsung, Motorola, Sony Ericsson but abandoned in 2013, as well as BlackBerry OS and Windows 10 Mobile from Microsoft (these two being no longer developed but still benefiting from maintenance), and finally two systems that equip phones and tablets today: Android and iOS.

Android, based on Linux, was developed by Google, and it dominates the market (86.8% market share in 2018 according to IDC Research) and is used by the majority of manufacturers. **iOS**, derived from macOS, equips Apple's hardware, with a 13.2% market share.

Some predict some convergence of laptops and tablets (hybrid computers). The first products available in 2018 are based on the OS of computers (Windows 10) or on the OS of tablets (iOS for Apple). In any case, it is very unlikely that new OSs will be developed in this context.

3.3.5.3. *Real-time operating systems*

As mentioned, real-time systems (RTOS for Real-Time Operating System) must respond in a finite and specified time to stimuli generated by the outside world. We will also talk about **embedded systems** for these components that integrate software and hardware and provide critical functionality with continuous interaction with their physical environment.

Two categories of real-time systems can be distinguished: "hard" real-time systems (the response of the system in time is vital, so it must be reliable and available in all circumstances), and "soft" real-time systems (time constraint overruns are tolerable within certain limits). They are generally broken down into subsystems with interacting tasks or processes, and their core must react very quickly to external events.

There are many real-time systems; here are four of them:

– **VxWorks**, developed by Wind River, is mainly used by research and industry (aeronautics, automotive, transportation). For example, NASA has used it in numerous space missions.

– **QNX** (originally called QUnix for Quick Unix) is designed primarily for the embedded systems market such as cars and industries. The company that develops it has been owned by BlackBerry since 2010.

– **OSEK/VDX** was created in 1993 by a consortium of German car manufacturers and equipment suppliers, later joined by Renault and PSA. Its aim is to meet the severe constraints of real-time execution of embedded software used in automotive electronics.

– **FreeRTOS** is a free and open-source real-time operating system. In 2017, the project and its team of developers were acquired by Amazon.

3.3.5.4. Operating systems for connected objects

Connected objects, such as smartphones, need an OS to function, but with two strong constraints: use as little memory as possible and consume as little power as possible.

There is not yet a dominant OS for all categories of connected objects, as the spectrum of sizes, uses and hardware configurations is so wide. However, the Linux kernel is, again, widely present and some real-time OSs may have lighter versions adapted to connected objects.

In late 2016, Google announced **Android Things**, an Android-derived platform designed to run on low-power devices. This announcement should be seen in a context where major international groups are seeking to capture the emerging market of the Internet of Things, a strategy that sometimes relies on a specific OS. While Microsoft is pinning all its hopes on **Windows 10 IoT**, Huawei seems to be pinning its hopes on **LiteOS**, an ultralight system (some cite a size of 10 Kbytes) for connected objects, while Samsung supports **Tizen**, based on Linux and developed in collaboration with Intel.

3.4. "High-level" programming and applications

Remember that the "high-level" programming languages are located in the layer above the operating system layer. They therefore essentially concern applications.

We will discuss some of these languages, positioning them according to the principles that have guided their development. The **programming paradigm** will be discussed as a way to approach computer programming and to deal with solutions to problems and their formulation in an appropriate programming language. Each paradigm is defined by a set of programming concepts.

There are four main programming paradigms:

– **mandatory** (or procedural) **programming** describes operations in sequence of instructions executed by the computer. It is the oldest paradigm;

– **object programming** consists of defining and assembling software components called objects (such as Java and Ada);

– **functional programming** in which a program is a function in the mathematical sense of the term (such as Lisp, Caml and Haskell);

– **declarative programming** consists of declaring the data of the problem and then asking the program to solve it. This is the case with HTML or XML.

Here are some of the languages that have marked or still mark the history of programming. They have, of course, evolved over time (versions, normalizations, etc.).

3.4.1. *Imperative languages*

The building blocks of mandatory programming are instruction sequences, loops and switches. We talk about sequential execution. The program tells the machine precisely what it must do (imperative orders) and efficiency is sought.

It is, historically, the basis of the first programming languages. We can retain some languages.

Fortran (Formula Translator) was founded in 1957 by John Backus from IBM. It was intended to provide scientists with a simple means of moving from arithmetic expressions to an effective program. It is very efficient in the field of numerical computation and has been the subject of several standardizations over the decades to exploit the new possibilities of computers (vectorization, coprocessors, parallelism). It is still used in major scientific applications.

Cobol (Common Business Oriented Language) was created in 1959 in response to a request from the US government for a manufacturer-independent programming language to manage the US administration. It was designed to create business applications and added the concepts of record and structured files. It is still used today, after several standardized revisions, for example in banks.

PL/1 (Programming Language number 1) was developed by IBM in the early 1960s. Its objective was to be universal and to be able to replace languages for scientific (Fortran) or commercial (Cobol) purposes. The programmers of each of these two languages did not appreciate the additions made for the other language, which did not allow PL/1 to take the place it should have taken (I myself greatly appreciated the efficiency of PL/1 at the end of the 1970s!).

C is an imperative and general-purpose language that was created in 1972 at Bell Laboratories, by Dennis Ritchie and Ken Thompson, for the development of the Unix system. Some consider it a lower level language than the three previous languages because its instructions are closer to the machine and the user has to program certain processes that are automatically supported in the higher level languages. The power of C – fast, portable and general-purpose – has ensured its continued success. It has influenced many newer languages including C++, Java and PHP.

Without being exhaustive, we should also mention languages that have had a significant place in the past: **Algol** (Algorithmic Oriented Language), created in 1958 but which has not been commercially successful; **Pascal**, a descendant of Algol created in 1968 by Niklaus Wirth; **APL** (A Programming Language), created in 1962 by Ken Iverson and which has been widely used in applied mathematics.

3.4.2. *Functional languages*

A functional language is a language in which the notion of function (procedure, subprogram) is central. A program is no longer a series of instructions to be executed but a composition of functions. This definition covers so-called pure functional languages, in which any calculation is performed by means of function calls (Haskell or Coq, for example) and imperative functional languages (Lisp, ML).

Their proximity to mathematical formalism is a major asset of these languages, because this feature makes it easier to prove, than in the imperative paradigm, that programs achieve what they were designed for.

Lisp (List Processing) is the oldest family of programming languages that is both imperative and functional. Lisp was born out of the need for a symbolic programming language that performs well in symbol reasoning rather than in numerical information processing. It was created in 1958 at MIT by John McCarthy, one of the founders of artificial intelligence. Lisp consists of functions to be evaluated and not of procedures to be executed like procedural languages. Lisp was followed by many versions like Common Lisp and is used in industry (robotics), aeronautics (NASA), etc.

Caml (Categorical Abstract Machine Language) is a general-purpose programming language that falls into the category of functional languages, as well as lends itself to imperative (and object-oriented) programming for OCaml. Descendant of the ML (Meta Language) language created by Robin Milner in the 1970s at the University of Edinburgh, it has been developed since 1985 by Inria, designed to create secure and reliable programs. The functional style brings the Caml language closer to mathematical writing. Numerous extensions of Caml allow the language to cover various concepts.

Haskell is a pure functional programming language, created in 1990 by a committee of language theory researchers interested in functional languages and "lazy" evaluation (the program will not perform the functions until it is forced to provide the results). Haskell has evolved a lot and now has very efficient compilers like GHC (Glasgow Haskell Compiler).

3.4.3. *Object programming*

Object-Oriented Programming (OOP) consists of the definition and assembly of software bricks called objects. The definition (or structure) of an object describes the characteristics of the object, an object (or instance) being the concrete realization of the object's structure. We can say that OOP is a way of developing an application that consists of representing (also called modeling) a computer application in the form of objects with properties that can interact with each other. Various languages allow this approach, although the most important are not limited to this paradigm, which was introduced in the 1970s by Alan Kay, who worked in the Xerox laboratories in Palo Alto.

Ada, the first version of which dates back to 1983, was designed following a call for tenders from the US Department of Defense (DoD), according to very strict specifications, by a French team led by Frenchman Jean Ichbiah. The Ada 95 version was an internationally standardized object language. It is used in real-time and embedded systems that require a high level of reliability and security: avionics, military uses, etc.

C++ was created in 1983 by Bjarne Stroustrup. From version 2.0 of the C language, it is a programming language allowing programming under multiple paradigms. Like C, it is a so-called "low-level" language because it is closer to the operation of the machine, which makes it particularly efficient. Its good performance and compatibility with C make it one of the most widely used programming languages for performance-critical applications.

Java, created by Sun Microsystems, was officially created in 1995. It has many advantages such as being portable, meaning that a program made in Java can be run on different platforms such as Windows, MacOS and Linux. This portability is due to the fact that this language is not compiled in machine code but it is compiled in an intermediate language called ByteCode. It then requires what is called a Java Virtual Machine (JVM) to run it. Only this virtual machine changes depending on the system. The Java language is popular mainly because it is the basis of most networked applications. Java technology can be found in all areas: laptops, game consoles, scientific supercomputers, cell phones, etc.

JavaScript was created in 1995 by the American Brendan Eich who was working at that time for Netscape, creator of the first popular web browser. It is a programming language of scripts (sequences of instructions that will be interpreted by a program) mainly used in interactive web pages, so it is an essential part of web applications. JavaScript should not be confused with the Java language invented at the same time; their syntaxes are close, but their uses and philosophies are very different.

Python is an interpreted, portable, dynamic, extensible, free language that allows a modular and object-oriented approach to programming. Python has been developed since 1989 and many volunteer contributors have improved it over time. Python is suitable for scripts of a dozen lines as well as complex projects of tens of thousands of lines. Python's syntax is very simple and, combined with advanced data types (lists, dictionaries, etc.), leads to programs that are both very compact and very readable.

C# is an object-oriented language created by Microsoft in 2002. Derived from C++ and very close to Java, it is intended to develop many applications, especially web applications. It is part of a larger set, known as the Microsoft .NET Framework. C# is increasingly seen as a competitor to the Java language.

3.4.4. *Other programming languages*

Other languages have been created, thanks to research work and to respond to new needs.

Prolog (an acronym for the French for logical programming: *programmation logique*) was created by Alain Colmerauer and Philippe Roussel in the early 1970s. It is a declarative programming language for solving logical problems. The principle of logical programming is to describe the statement of a problem by a set of expressions and logical links and allow the compiler to transform it into a sequence of instructions. Prolog is used in artificial intelligence and computer language processing.

Esterel is a precursor of synchronous reactive languages for applications whose function is to constantly interact with their environment (aircraft, robotics, autonomous vehicles, etc.). Based on signals, it was created in the 1980s by Gérard Berry's team at Sophia-Antipolis. Together with Lustre, another synchronous reactive language, it became SCADE, which is developed industrially by the company Esterel Technologies.

Finally, even though we are not talking about programming languages in the strict sense of the word, we should mention two languages associated with the Web: **HTML** (Hypertext Markup Language) already mentioned in Chapter 2, and **PHP** (Hypertext Preprocessor), created by Rasmus Lerdorf in 1994, a scripting language mainly used to produce dynamic web pages.

3.4.5. *The most used languages*

We have seen some languages, but there are many others, and new languages are appearing.

The IEEE (Institute of Electrical and Electronics Engineers), a reference organization in the field of information and communication technologies, publishes a list each year of the languages considered to be the most important. Figure 3.5 gives the IEEE[2] 2018 list.

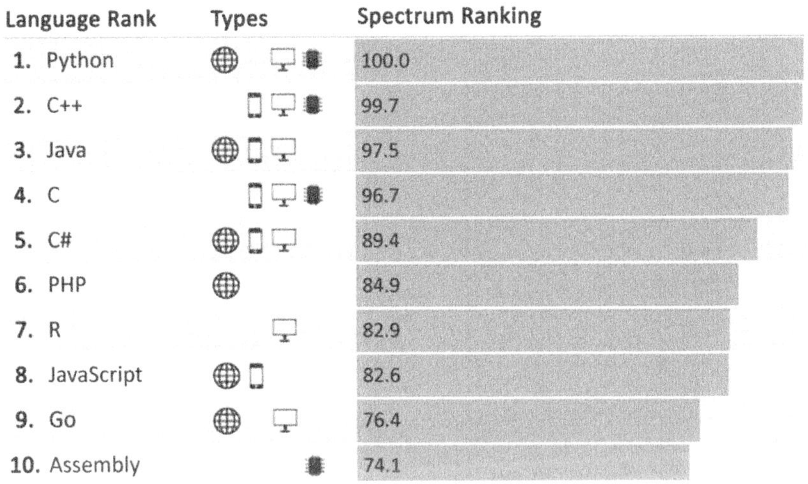

Language Rank	Types	Spectrum Ranking
1. Python	⊕ 🖥 ▮	100.0
2. C++	▯ 🖥 ▮	99.7
3. Java	⊕ ▯ 🖥	97.5
4. C	▯ 🖥 ▮	96.7
5. C#	⊕ ▯ 🖥	89.4
6. PHP	⊕	84.9
7. R	🖥	82.9
8. JavaScript	⊕ ▯	82.6
9. Go	⊕ 🖥	76.4
10. Assembly	▮	74.1

Figure 3.5. *The most commonly used languages*

---

2 https://spectrum.ieee.org/static/interactive-the-top-programming-languages-2018.

We note that the applications associated with communicating computing have a very strong impact in this ranking.

3.5. Software development

3.5.1. *Software categories*

Software is commonly classified into two categories: system software and application software.

System software includes, in addition to the operating system, **utility software**. While closely related to the operating system, it is not part of it. These utilities include file managers (backup, compression, archiving, version management, etc.), disk managers (de-fragmentation, cleaning, etc.), security software (antivirus), communication software (browser, search engine, e-mail), PDF or audio file reading software, etc.

Although the utility software that comes with operating systems is becoming increasingly comprehensive and sophisticated, users often install third-party utility software as a replacement for or in addition to the utility software that comes with the operating system.

Unlike system software, **application software** (often referred to as **apps**) is chosen by the user to meet his or her own needs or to perform special processing. Included among these apps are the following:

– office software: word processing, spreadsheets, etc.;

– database management systems (we will come back to this in Chapter 4);

– applications related to business management: accounting, personnel management, inventory, etc.;

– computer-aided design applications: industry, architecture, electronics, etc.;

– applications in the pedagogical field: computer-assisted teaching, MOOC, etc.;

– gaming software;

– software that you or I have developed for our specific needs or just for pleasure.

3.5.2. *Software quality*

The development of software often represents a significant investment involving many people, from project managers to IT specialists and to users. The aim is therefore to produce software with a high level of quality. For their part, software companies are looking for a standard to guarantee the quality of the products they offer to potential customers. But what are the criteria for defining quality? Organizations developing large software products have been working on this subject for a long time.

The ISO 9126 standard, "Software engineering – Product quality", defines and describes a series of quality characteristics of a software product. It was published in 1991 and revised in 2001. The SQuaRE (Software Quality Requirements and Evaluation) standard, defined since 2005, is the successor to the ISO 9126 standard.

The SQuaRE model consists of eight characteristics, broken down into subcharacteristics, each of which must have a precise definition. If you, reader of this book, are developing software, think about these characteristics:

– **functional adequacy**: degree to which a product or system provides functions that meet stated and implied needs when used under specified conditions;

– **performance efficiency**: performance relative to the amount of resources used under stated conditions (response time, use of resources);

– **compatibility**: degree to which a product, system or component can exchange information with other products, systems or components, and/or perform its required functions, while sharing the same hardware or software environment;

– **usability**: degree to which a product or system can be used by specified users to achieve specified goals with effectiveness, efficiency and satisfaction, in a specified context of use;

– **reliability**: degree to which a system, product or component performs specified functions under specified conditions (maturity, availability, fault tolerance);

– **security**: degree to which a product or system protects information and data so that people or other products have the degree of data access appropriate to their types and levels of authorization;

– **maintainability**: degree of effectiveness and efficiency with which a product or system can be modified by the intended maintainers;

– **portability**: degree of effectiveness and efficiency with which a system, product or component can be transferred from one hardware, software or other operational or usage environment to another.

3.5.3. *Development methods*

The term **software development** is used to refer to all activities related to the creation of software and the programs that make it up, **programming** being the part corresponding to the writing of the programs themselves. The main stages of software production, whatever they may be, are the following:

– **needs analysis**: general objectives, future system environment, available resources, performance constraints, etc. It is mainly the responsibility of the client/user;

– **software specifications**: clear description of what the software should do (detailed functionalities, quality requirements, interfaces, etc.). They must be the subject of a detailed specification listing functional and non-functional requirements;

– **general design**: to elaborate a concrete solution realizing the specification. Architectural description in components (with interfaces and functionalities);

– **detailed design**: realization of functionalities by components (algorithms, data organization) and non-functional requirements (performance, security, etc.);

– **programming**: choice of development environment, programming language(s), development standards, coding;

– **verification**: tests on the different components and on the whole product;

– **validation**: ensuring that the client's needs are met.

Software development specialists have always sought to formalize methods to make this work more efficient and provide a result in line with the needs expressed by the user (the client). Here are two methods that show two slightly different approaches.

3.5.3.1. *The V-model*

The V-model is a well-known organizational method that was adapted to computers in the 1980s. It is one of the first methods learned at school and it is still used today.

The V-model is a cycle composed of three main phases: **design** (from the analysis of the needs expressed by the user to the detailed design), **implementation** (coding and unit tests of the different modules), and **validation** (the software components are integrated into the final solution to check that the integration does not cause any anomalies). The product is then tested against the functional specifications and validated before going into production.

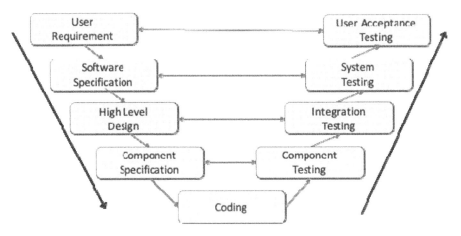

Figure 3.6. *The V-shaped development model*

The V-model method is based on the principle that the client already knows all the features he or she needs and that he or she will not change his or her mind during development. In addition, it is often during product implementation that conceptual problems are identified. The main flaw of this method is therefore its lack of flexibility. It is particularly for these reasons that many IT projects are stopped along the way, and others end up costing a lot more than they could have if they had been delivered on time and on budget, while offering fewer features than required.

3.5.3.2. *The AGILE cycle*

To give flexibility to the development process, the AGILE method proposes a completely different approach: project management by **iterative cycle**. This approach considers that the need to which the software must respond cannot be fixed, and it proposes, on the contrary, to adapt to changes in the software.

The customer and the service provider will define together an overall objective to be reached, as well as the organization and functioning of the project team. Then, several steps leading to this objective are determined. Finally, each of these steps will be divided into tasks to be handled by the development team. The software is thus developed step by step, each of which must be validated before moving on to the next step, until the overall objective is reached.

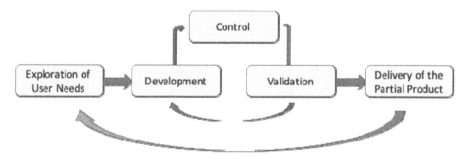

Figure 3.7. *AGILE: iterations batch by batch*

The AGILE method is flexible (users and developers have to work together throughout the project); it is reassuring because the client sees developments as they happen; it is fast because the customer can use the system even though all the functionalities are not yet implemented.

3.5.4. *Software engineering*

The production of software is complex and poor quality (from insufficient verification and validation, cost and time overruns, etc.) can have serious consequences. Numerous failures have easily shown that this production must be based on systematic, rigorous and measurable procedures to ensure that the specification corresponds to the client's real needs and that the deadlines and costs allocated to the production are respected.

Software engineering can be defined as the set of methods, techniques and tools dedicated to the design, development and maintenance of computer software. We could say that it is the art of building software industrially.

Software engineering is not only concerned with the technical aspects of analysis and design, but also with the entire software lifecycle – needs analysis, design, maintenance, testing, certification, standardization, deployment – as well as organizational aspects (team building, process management, forecasting and monitoring of costs and deadlines). Project management is a complement to software engineering.

Various standardization bodies (AFNOR, IEEE, etc.) have published recommendations and standards to be applied in software engineering, and many software engineering training courses exist and are tending to multiply.

3.6. Software verification and validation

3.6.1. *Errors with sometimes tragic consequences*

We have seen that software is everywhere. In particular, we find it in the embedded systems that have now invaded our daily lives: smartphones and tablets, car navigation, bank cards, multimedia (photo, video, music), etc. This software sometimes contains millions of lines of code and we are obliged to trust them (when I press the brake pedal of my car, I do not wonder if the software that will manage braking has been well designed and made!).

In all the development cycles seen above, the test phases are crucial. Indeed, a software malfunction can have catastrophic consequences and, moreover, it will generate high costs since the defect will have to be corrected.

The term "bug" is used both to designate a defect introduced into the software during one of the phases of the development cycle and an anomaly in the expected behavior. The term bug comes from a tasty anecdote: in 1947, an insect got stuck in a relay of the Mark II computer at Harvard University, causing a failure!

One of the most famous quality defects is the one that affected Flight 501, the inaugural flight of the European launcher Ariane 5, which took place on June 4, 1996. It resulted in a failure, caused by a malfunction in the data processing, which saw the rocket explode in flight only 36.7 seconds after lift-off. Several problems of software non-quality were at the origin of this spectacular mistake. The portion of code at the origin of the failure had in fact been taken from an old system (in this case Ariane 4), and was unfortunately not adapted to the power of its successor. The cost of this mistake was several hundred million euros!

The automotive industry is not spared from defects in its embedded software. For example, in 2013, and based on an expert report on the software managing the acceleration system, a US jury judged for the first time that design problems in the embedded software on the Toyota Camry were responsible for the uncontrolled acceleration of the vehicle, which resulted in the death of a passenger.

The verification of software based on numerical models (avionics, weather, etc.) is particularly tricky because of the accuracy of the data handled (number of digits, rounding, etc.). From the implementation of arithmetic in programs to the actual specification of tasks, the sources of error are multiple. For example, the Mars Climate Orbiter probe crashed on Mars in September 1999 due to a staggering blunder: some of the software designers assumed that the unit of measurement was the meter, and others assumed that it was the foot.

But mistakes are not always human. A compiler translates a program into machine language, but a bug in the compiler can lead to false machine code. This is also true of operating systems, which are very complex and therefore prone to bugs (you may have noticed this with the OS of your personal computer). Errors can even occur in the processors themselves, as was the case in the floating division operation (an operation in which dividend and divisor are real numbers, not integers) of the Intel Pentium processor in 1994.

Readers interested in other examples of defects that have had serious consequences can refer to Gérard Berry's excellent book, *L'Hyperpuissance de l'informatique* (Berry 2017).

Experts in the field estimate that in Europe, losses due to programming errors cost more than 100 billion euros per year.

3.6.2. Software testing

Software testing is the process of analyzing a program against its specifications with the intention of detecting possible anomalies in order to validate it. It is the oldest and most widely used method, still used today. In the software development process, almost half of the effort is spent on **verification** testing (does the system do its job properly?) and **validation** testing (does the system produced correspond to the customer's needs?).

There are generally two types of tests, namely **static** and **dynamic testing**. Static testing is done without running the software (in part or in full). This is the case for code or specification inspection reviews, done by specialists. The dynamic test, on the contrary, consists of testing a system by running it with real input data and this is what we are going to specify.

Regardless of its type, the test is effective in finding errors, but it cannot prove that there are no errors.

3.6.2.1. Qualification of tests

Without going into detail about the classification of tests, we will limit ourselves to giving the four levels of testing identified by the French Committee for Software Testing (*Comité français du test logiciel*, CFTL): **component** (testing of small parts of the code, separately), **integration** (testing of a set of parts of the code that cooperate, testing of modules together), **system** (testing of the entire system, inspecting its functionality) and **acceptance** (acceptance by the user).

It is also necessary to ensure the non-regression tests, which consist of verifying that the correction of the errors has not affected the parts already tested (the tests already executed must be systematically repeated).

Manual or automatic tests? We can distinguish:

– manual tests: the tester enters the test data, runs the tests, observes the results and compares them to the expected results. This is tedious and unmanageable for large applications;

– automated testing with tool support that relieves the tester of launching tests and recording results. Automatic test case generation tools are becoming more and more common;

– tests built into the software itself: these are lines of code added to an application to perform run-time checks.

These verification and validation activities are most often done under the responsibility of a testing professional because the program developer is not in the best position to verify the program's quality.

3.6.2.2. *Testing strategy and plan*

A program usually has a very large number of possible executions and it is impossible to validate all of them. It is therefore necessary to define a test strategy to be as relevant as possible. This strategy must be integrated into the software development process. It depends on the criticality of the software (seriousness of the consequences of a possible anomaly) and the cost of software development; it defines the resources required (human resources, tools) and the criteria used to establish whether each element of the software has succeeded or failed.

The test plan identifies the objectives and the means to carry out the tests. It allows the technical organization of the tests, defining what will be tested, why to test, how and when the tests will be carried out, and who will test. The goal is to establish the order in which each component is ready, tested individually, and integrated with the other components of the system. It also serves as a validation document for the final quality of the software and is part of the project contract documents, along with the technical specifications or functional requirements. It is designed by the test manager and validated by the project manager.

3.6.2.3. *What guarantees?*

Testing, no matter how extensive, cannot guarantee that a software program is bug-free, especially if it is a "big" piece of software in terms of lines of code.

Software publishers are well aware of this and therefore include clauses in user licenses that exclude the guarantee of conformity. The user therefore accepts the software as is.

Specific software developers, for their part, often offer free bug fixes for a limited period of time.

A legal action based on the existence of a latent defect can only be invoked if the purchaser proves that the malfunction is due to a defect that is both hidden and serious, which in the IT field can be difficult. The tests therefore do not guarantee anything.

We will see another approach, that of formal methods, which tries to guarantee the absence of bugs.

3.6.3. *Formal methods*

3.6.3.1. *The formal methods approach*

Software is everywhere and can be millions of lines of code. Their vulnerability to both design and programming errors as well as to malicious use requires that their verification and validation be pushed to the limit, as they can put human lives at risk.

The difficulty of making programs right is a well-known problem. The first approach, which is the oldest and which we have gone through, relies on software engineering and the use of tests. However, the cost of these tests can be very high and they provide no guarantees.

Another approach, much more scientific, is to use mathematical tools to specify, validate and verify computer systems. These mathematically based approaches are commonly referred to as **formal methods**. Researchers have long imagined giving a mathematical meaning to a program, the choice of mathematics being explained by the need for rigor and precision in describing the behavior of complex systems.

Formal methods are computer techniques of great rigor that, with the help of specialized languages and logical rules, ensure (ideally) the absence of any defect in computer programs. The main elements of a formal method are:

– a formal language for writing specifications;

– rules for assessing the validity and quality of specifications;

– strategies and rules for refining specifications and verifying these refinements (in computer science, refinement consists of having a design approach where the level of detail is refined at each step).

Generally, a formal specification describes what is to be done (what?) without saying how it will be done (how?). It prescribes a property that is deemed necessary to obtain. Its statement may be a function, capability, characteristic or limitation that a system, product or process must satisfy.

A simple specification consists of defining the types of data that will be manipulated in the software, which will enable checking their consistency. For example, the cosine function cannot be applied to character data. Checking that the software manipulates the data in coherence with its type allows errors to be detected, even before the software itself is executed.

Formal methods can be applied at different stages of the system development process, from specification through verification to final implementation. Automation of the refinement process speeds up software development by entrusting a tool with the mechanical transformation of a complete abstract model into an installable model.

Formal verification of a system also assumes that the tools used, such as a compiler, have been formally verified. With this in mind, Xavier Leroy and his team at Inria developed the CompCert compiler for the C language, entirely written and proven with the Coq software, a tool for writing and verifying programs also developed at Inria under the direction of Gérard Huet.

This approach can be summarized with the three stages presented in Figure 3.8, for which verification tools can be used.

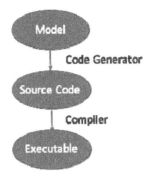

Figure 3.8. *The formal methods approach*

This approach using formal methods challenges traditional development cycles, and in particular the V-model described above.

3.6.3.2. *B method*

Invented by the Frenchman Jean-Raymond Abrial in the mid-1990s, the formal B method is an approach that makes it possible to specify and design software while ensuring its safety and reliability. Thus, the whole specification, design and coding process is entirely based on the realization of a certain number of mathematical evidence.

The formal B method evokes the set comprising the B-language, refinement, evidence and associated tools. It has been successfully used for several industrial applications, and includes several development steps:

– describe needs: abstract specification;

– check that everything is said consistently;

– head towards implementation by successive refinement;

– proving at each step that the properties remain valid.

The embedded software of the automatic control system for line 14 of the Paris metro (METEOR) was thus developed using the B method. Since its first tests in 1997, its safety systems (86,000 lines of code, which have been proven to comply with the original specifications) have not experienced any failures.

3.6.3.3. *The future*

Even though industrial tools are now available to implement this approach with a sufficient degree of maturity, the use of formal methods is still not widespread and their large-scale use will still require investment in research, as well as in the training of computer scientists.

3.6.4. *Software certification*

Certification is a procedure by which a software publisher obtains the attestation of compliance with a quality standard. In general, certification authorizes the use of a label, such as the NF label. Certification bodies are independent and follow long and rigorous processes before awarding a certification to a software, whereas a certificate issued by the software publisher means that it has paid particular attention to compliance with standards in the design of its software.

Measuring software quality is more complex than it seems. First, it is necessary to clearly define what the word quality means for each company, each team and each piece of software being measured. Once the quality objectives have been clearly established, the next step is to know how to measure them. Different models exist for measuring quality, but none, to my knowledge, has defined a clear standard to provide official certification.

It is not simple to measure the quality of a word processing software package, for example, from the characteristics of the SQuaRE model. However, this has not prevented the implementation of certifications for specific software that must comply with very strong constraints, particularly legal ones. The NF software certification is undoubtedly the best known and is a mark for software professionals.

Since the entry into force of the VAT anti-fraud law on January 1, 2018, publishers and users of cash register software have not been able to miss this certification. Cash management software has the obligation to meet the conditions of inalterability, security, conservation and archiving of data. The certification, in this particular case as well as in the case of accounting software, first focuses on the characteristics "functional adequacy", "reliability" and "security".

In another field, that of health, the *Haute autorité de santé* in France is in charge of establishing certification procedures for healthcare professionals' software (prescription assistance software, dispensing assistance software, database on medicines). In particular, it draws up reference systems containing all the requirements to be met.

The work carried out by numerous research teams should lead to metrics that will enable the precise conditions for certification to be defined with a global quality reference system. However, development through formal methods is a recognized approach.

3.7. Legal protection and distribution of software

Software is therefore a set of programs accompanied by everything necessary to make it operational. The creators of software are, for the most part, companies called software publishers. The software market represents considerable economic stakes. According to Syntec Numérique, one of the France's professional associations in the digital industry, it represented more than 13 billion euros for France in 2016.

Software is a work that has a cost (the means used to create it) and a value (that stems from the service it provides, from the expertise contained within the source code). It is useful to understand how software can be protected (against piracy or counterfeiting, for example) and under what conditions it can be used by others.

So we are going to cover a little bit of software law, trying not to be too boring, before describing the main modes of distribution.

3.7.1. *Legal protection of software*

In France, the Intellectual Property Code (*Code de la propriété intellectuelle*, CPI) is the legal corpus that brings together all the laws and regulations relating to intellectual property and aimed at protecting "works of the mind". It is divided into two branches:

– **literary and artistic property** which, as its name indicates, concerns literary works (novels, short stories, plays, etc.) and artistic works (paintings, drawings, sculptures, etc.). It is composed of copyright and neighboring rights;

– **industrial property**, which aims to protect trademarks, patentable inventions, designs and models, and thus prevent counterfeiting.

The software is protected in France by copyright, but it has been adapted to the software in order to understand its technical aspect. Ideas are not protected under French law; this is the case for algorithms. On the contrary, the programs (source code and object code) are protected, as well as the user documentation.

Copyright confers two types of rights:

– the moral right that protects the author's non-economic interests; attached to the author, it is inalienable and perpetual;

– economic rights that allow the rights holder to receive remuneration for the exploitation of his works by third parties. They are limited in time and can be transferred to a third party.

Economic rights have been adapted for software. The essential point is that these rights are automatically transferred to the employer when the authors have developed the software as part of an employed activity. It is the employer who alone decides on the life of the work (distribution, choice of license, etc.). Authors who are not paid employees remain holders of the economic rights on their software works and can transfer these rights to third parties under the conditions of their choice.

The protection is automatic; it is acquired as soon as the software is designed. If one wishes to validate this protection in a more formal way in the event of litigation, it is prudent to pre-constitute proof of paternity and anteriority. This can be done, for example, by filing with a notary, or with a specialized association such as the French Agency for the Protection of Programs (*Agence pour la protection des programmes*, APP).

3.7.2. *Licenses*

Buying contains the idea of transfer of ownership (you buy a car, it becomes your property). When you purchase or download software to your personal computer, you do not buy the software, even though it is free; you sign a contract allowing you to use it. The license is an offer of contract from the supplier, which defines the conditions of use of this software (so it is important to read the content of the license, even though we do not always do it!). Anyone using, copying, modifying or distributing software without explicit permission of the holder of the economic rights is guilty of counterfeiting.

There are many types of software licenses:

– proprietary software: all rights are reserved by their owner. This is the case for the vast majority of commercial software. The software is generally distributed only in binary form (without source code) with very strict usage constraints: limited use, no right to copy or modify the software, etc.;

– shareware: private software that can be used free of charge for a short period of time or a limited number of times. Then, the use of the software becomes a paying one;

– freeware: private software that is free of charge but does not necessarily give rights (other than the right to use it) such as including access to the source code and sometimes even redistribution;

– free software: software that gives many rights to its users, but it is not necessarily free of charge. We will discuss this type of license at greater length, because it is interesting and has developed considerably over the last 30 years.

3.7.3. *Free software and open source*

The notion of **free software** was first described in the early 1980s by Richard Stallman, a researcher at MIT, who then formalized and popularized it with the GNU project and the Free Software Foundation (FSF).

Free software has four freedoms in common:

– freedom to run the program for any purpose;

– freedom to redistribute copies of the program received;

– freedom to study the functioning of the program and to adapt it to its needs (which implies access to the program's source code);

– freedom to redistribute the program modified by the user (which allows the mutualization of developments).

Free software does not necessarily imply free of charge; the FSF's maxim on this point is "free as in free speech, not as in free beer". However, this onerous nature should not restrict the freedoms provided by the license.

Born in 1998 from a split in the free software community in order to conduct a policy deemed more adapted to economic and technical realities, the open-source movement defends the freedom to access the sources of the programs used, in order to achieve a software economy dependent solely on the sale of services and no longer on the sale of user licenses.

However, it is not easy to tell the difference between free software and open source. According to Richard Stallman, the fundamental difference between the two concepts lies in their philosophy: "Open source is a development methodology; free software is a social movement." In practice, most open-source licenses meet the FSF's criteria for open-source software, with the various subtleties that distinguish them being mainly philosophical and commercial.

There are many free or open-source licenses. The most widely used license is the GNU GPL (General Public License). Many free or open-source licenses are close to each other; some are compatible with each other, others have real philosophical differences. In particular, some licenses have a "contaminating" effect. For example, if a developer integrates a programming library published under GPL version 2, he or she must publish his or her software under the same license, and therefore publish his or her sources. Hence, the importance of reading the license that comes with the software!

3.8. The software market

Software represents a considerable market both economically and in terms of jobs. Here are a few figures to better measure the importance of this sector.

According to Gartner Inc., global corporate spending on software was $419 billion in 2018. These expenditures included licenses acquired from software publishers (companies that design, develop and market software products) and development done in-house or outsourced to DSCs (Digital Services Companies). The United States largely dominates these activities, with IBM and Microsoft being the top two producers.

Cloud computing (Software as a Service) is disrupting the world of software publishers as more and more companies are renting software services on the Cloud instead of purchasing expensive licenses. The revenue associated with these services is estimated to account for around 10% of global software spending.

Note that the open-source market is in very good health according to ReportBuyer. Its worldwide revenues are expected to increase from $11.40 billion in 2017 to $32.95 billion in 2022, an average annual growth rate of 23.65%.

In their report on the top 250 French software publishers (*TOP 250 des éditeurs de logiciels français,* 2019), Syntec Numérique and EY showed that this sector was particularly dynamic. Indeed, the market is booming with a 12% increase compared to 2016, representing a total of 16 billion euros in revenues for the 300 companies consulted. In addition, this strong dynamic led to the creation of 12,700 jobs between 2016 and 2018. Innovation is at the heart of the development strategy of software publishers, as they devote 14% of their revenues to R&D. Leading the way are Dassault Systèmes (3D design, digital 3D modeling), Criteo (Internet advertising targeting for brands and advertisers) and Ubisoft (video games).

Data: From Binary Element to Intelligence

4.1. Introduction

Since the Hollerith machine census of the American population in 1890, mentioned in Chapter 1, data have changed considerably in quantity, representation and diversity. But what do we mean by "data"?

A bit can be used to represent the numbers 0 and 1, the logical values true or false, that is, very little. We will therefore associate several bits in order to represent or code more consequent data.

A data, a set of bits, has no meaning in itself. It must be interpreted in a specific context to derive information from it. Is it a color code, a first name or an instruction in an assembly language?

The accumulation of coherent data leads to knowledge in a particular domain. It allows the interpretation of information for decision-making and action initiation. To take a simple example, the set of couples "dish, price" gives knowledge of the menu offered by a restaurant to order from it.

At the most elaborate stage, the analysis of a body of knowledge leads to intelligence, since it is a question of exploiting this knowledge with a precise objective.

A layered diagram (see Figure 4.1) can be used, as was done in Chapter 3.

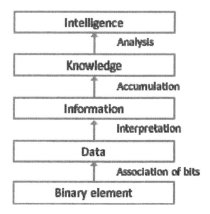

Figure 4.1. *From binary element to intelligence*

This chapter attempts to take a look at what we generally call data.

4.2. Data and information

We will start from the bit, because the basis of computing is a digital world. It was the American mathematician Claude Shannon, already mentioned, who in 1948 popularized the use of the word bit as an elementary measure of digital information.

The data are the work object of data processing. A data is a raw element, which has not yet been interpreted or put into context. It can be recorded, stored and transmitted.

Information is interpreted data. A number can represent a price, a temperature, etc. In other words, putting data in context creates added value to constitute information.

4.2.1. *Digitization of data*

As we saw in Chapter 1, data must be digitized to be understandable and manipulable by computers. Digitization is a process that allows objects (text, images, sounds, signals, etc.) to be represented by sequences of binary numbers (0 and 1). Let us see some examples of digitization.

4.2.1.1. *Characters*

The ASCII code (American Standard Code for Information Interchange) is one of the oldest codes used in computing. Initially based on 7 bits, it had to be extended to take into account accented characters among others. The need to be able to code multiple alphabets has led to the definition of new codes such as Unicode. The coexistence of these standards still presents problems, and we can see it in the e-mails we receive when an accented character is represented in a surprising way!

4.2.1.2. *Numbers*

A number is not a sequence of characters; it is a value that will enter into mathematical operations. The representation of numbers, in binary, depends on the type of number, and we will summarize the main representations.

The case of **natural numbers** is the simplest. The conversion to a bit string was explained in Chapter 1. If we code a 32-bit number (4 bytes), the maximum recordable integer (all bits are at 1) is $2^{32} - 1$.

The coding of **relative numbers** can be done by reserving a bit for the sign (+ or −). This method has drawbacks; however, representation by the complement to 2 offers a solution. To apply this, we change 0 into 1 and 1 into 0 in the binary number, and add 1 to the result. For example, if the number 6 is 0110 in binary, the complement to 2 is 1010. The result of the addition x + (− x) is zero! The first bit (most significant bit) of a negative number is always equal to 1, and we only have to make additions.

A **real number** is a number that can be represented by a whole part and a sequence of decimals, for example, −37.5 in decimal form. On a computer, floating-point numbers are generally used. In decimal form, −37.5 can be written as -0.375×10^2, the general form being s × m × e, where s is the sign, m is the mantissa and e is the exhibitor. To represent a real number over 32 bits, we can have 1 bit for the sign, 8 bits for the exponent and 23 bits for the mantissa.

4.2.1.3. *Sound*

A sound is a continuous analog quantity represented by a curve varying with time. Digitization is carried out in two stages: **sampling** and **quantification**.

In **sampling**, the sound is cut into slices or samples. The sampling frequency corresponds to the number of samples per second. In order to translate the analog signal as accurately as possible, as many measurements as possible should be taken per second.

Each sample is then quantified, which gives a numerical value to the sound. The greater the sampling frequency, the closer the digital signal will be to the analog signal and therefore the better the digitization will be.

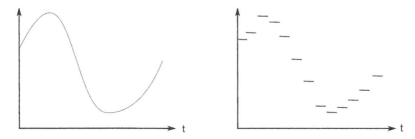

Figure 4.2. *Analog signal and digital signal*

4.2.1.4. *Images*

A digital image is composed of elementary units (called pixels), each of which represents a portion of the image. An image is defined by the number of pixels that constitute it in width and height, each pixel being a triplet of numbers (r,v,b) encoding the luminous intensity of red, green and blue in a color coding system. Digitizing a document consists of assigning a numerical value to each of these points.

We will return to images in Chapter 5.

4.2.1.5. *Many other types of data*

Data can be used as a variable in a computer program, and many types have emerged.

Metadata is data used to define or describe another piece of data (e.g. associating the date of capture and GPS coordinates with a photo).

A Java program can handle simple (or primitive)-type variables and complex-type variables (objects).

The Web has also brought a new approach to the notion of data.

4.2.2. *Data compression*

All digital cameras on the market have sensors with several million pixels. Each pixel takes up space in memory: for example, in 16 million color mode, the pixel sometimes occupies 32 bits (4 bytes). The storage of a large number of photos therefore poses volume problems.

If we look at a photo, we note that many contiguous pixels are identical. On the contrary, it is not vital to preserve every little detail that will not be perceived by the human senses anyway. We will therefore, using specific algorithms, compress the data corresponding to this image.

Many compression algorithms exist, each with its own particularity and especially a target data type. A distinction is made between **lossless compression algorithms** (which, after decompression, restore a sequence of bits that is strictly identical to the original) and **lossy compression algorithms** (the sequence of bits obtained after decompression is more or less close to the original, depending on the desired quality). The former are mainly used for the compression of text and certain types of images (medicine), and the latter for speech, music, images and video.

For still images, JPEG is a lossy compression mode, but it allows a file to be reduced to one tenth of its original size without any visual quality change. PNG, on the contrary, is a lossless mode that makes files larger. MPEG is a lossy compression format for video sequences. MP3 is a lossy compression format for sound.

4.3. The structuring of data towards information

In this approach to digitization, we have cited elemental data and more complex entities such as images or sound sequences. The structuring of data is important; it is an organization that makes it possible to create information. It also simplifies and improves the efficiency of information processing and exchange.

4.3.1. *Structured data*

These are data decomposed according to a formal scheme with constraints on data types.

An **array T** is a data structure that allows us to store a determined number of elements T[i] marked by an index i. All the elements of the array generally have the same basic type (integer, for example). A program will be able to manipulate an array more simply than a sequence of elements.

Figure 4.3. *An array*

Unlike an array, whose length must be determined, the elements of a **chained list** are distributed in memory and linked together by pointers. We can add and remove elements of a chained list at any place and at any time, without having to recreate the whole list.

Figure 4.4. *A chained list*

A **record** is a logical grouping of several variables into a single variable consisting, for example, of a person's name, address and telephone number. It can be treated as information.

Figure 4.5. *A record*

Numerous other data structures exist and are used in programming: stacks, trees, graphs, etc.

More generally, structured data can be controlled by repositories and presented in boxes that allow their interpretation and processing by humans and machines. Databases, which we will present in section 4.5, use structured data.

4.3.2. *Semi-structured data and the Web*

We have more and more heterogeneous information, without a formal description scheme.

Electronic messaging, social networks and the Web carry large amounts of data that are impossible to interpret because they do not have a clear structure.

If I send a message to a friend that contains the data:

```
Victor
Hugo
Notre Dame de Paris
François
Rabelais
Gargantua
```

he will only understand what it is about if he knows the subject of my message and French literature. Of course, a computer cannot do much without proper instructions.

If, on the other hand, I use tags to say what each of these data represents, I can transform them into information:

```
<table.
  <author>
      <first name>Victor>/first name>
      <surname>Hugo</surname>
      <title>Notre Dame de Paris</title>
  </author>
  <author>
      <first name>François</first name>
      <surname>Rabelais</surname>
      <title>Gargantua>/title>
  </author>
</table>
```

A program will be able to decode and process this information, which can be said to be semi-structured and can therefore be processed by many applications.

XML (Extensible Markup Language) is a standard that has been adopted by the W3C to complement HTML for data exchange on the Web. The strength of XML lies in its ability to describe any data domain through its extensibility. It enables structuring, setting the vocabulary and syntax of the data it will contain.

4.4. Files and their formats

Data can be created by a user, generated by devices such as sensors (e.g. temperature), automatically generated by a program itself or simply an object from the Web. They are all ultimately represented by 0s and 1s (binary representation). But a sequence of 0s and 1s does not tell us what they represent; it is the format that will allow it, and we have just seen formats for numbers and images. A format is therefore a particular way of representing data in a form that can be understood by a computer, whether the data is structured or semi-structured.

A file is a record of data stored in a computer. The most common is the file containing the text we have just entered and saved. We can reread it, modify it, send it, etc. It is an entity in its own right.

Consistent collections of data, such as those relating to people working in a company, can be recorded and stored in a memory, in the form of a file, just as one could do on a notebook or a set of sheets.

A file has a **name** that is used to identify and access its contents, often with a suffix (the **extension**, i.e. the last letters of the file name after the "."), which provides information about the file type and therefore the software used to manipulate it. There are hundreds, if not thousands, of file types, which differ by the nature of the content, the format, the software used to manipulate the content, and the use the computer makes of it. The file format is the convention by which information is digitized and organized in the file.

Because of its flexibility, the notion of format has allowed the development of a large number of so-called proprietary formats (their specifications are not public or their use is restricted by their owner), which has posed many problems. To solve them, standard formats have been proposed and validated worldwide, and there are currently hundreds of standard formats for all file types. Table 4.1 provides a short list of common formats.

TXT	File extension for a plaintext file (data that represent only characters of readable material). Its advantage is that it can be read on all platforms.
DOC	File extension associated with the Microsoft Office Word application.
SXW	File created with the word processor of the Open Office suite.
XLS	File created with the Excel spreadsheet.
HTML	A file containing text with HTML tags that will govern the presentation of the text by a web browser on a screen.
PDF	File readable by Acrobat Reader software available on all platforms.
ZIP	File containing compressed files made with compression software (Winzip, Power Archiver, etc.).
MP3	Coding format for digital audio, allowing a large reduction in file sizes when compared to uncompressed audio.
MPEG	Format that compresses videos using the fact that some scenes are fixed or not very animated. There are several MPEG standards.
JPG JPEG	Compressed image format. Most image processing software gives the user a choice of compression ratio by allowing the user to see the effect of compression on the image.
TIFF	Universal image format recognized by all computer platforms. This format is more sophisticated than JPEG and has more options.

Table 4.1. *Common file formats*

We have moved from isolated information to knowledge, with these consistent data collections providing an essential additional level of information. But we are going to progress further in the level of knowledge.

4.5. Databases

4.5.1. *The main characteristics*

For years, files have been the most common way to organize and store data.

As more and more data become available, managing and using them can pose many problems. Let us take the example of a company's human resources department. It needs to have a complete list of employees with their identity, their employment contract, the unit to which each one is assigned, their index (to establish the salary), etc. The data can be used to establish the salary of each employee. Some information changes (family situation, unit of assignment, etc.). The unit manager needs additional information (e.g. holiday). The department in charge of training needs to know the development of each person's career. The multiplicity of files results in redundant data, which makes it difficult to update. In addition, the needs of the users of these data are diverse and subject to change. A solution must therefore be found.

A database (DB) is an entity in which it is possible to store data in a structured way and with as little redundancy as possible. These data, which are described in the database itself, must be able to be used by different programs and users. The distinction between the physical level and the logical level is essential, and a last level provides the views that users can have of these data.

A database makes it possible to make data available to users for consultation, entry or updating, while ensuring the rights granted to the latter. The standard approach in databases is based on a client–server architecture: the client (person or program) sends a request to the server, this request is compiled and executed, and the response is sent to the client by the server.

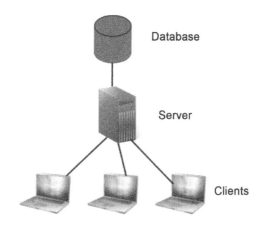

Figure 4.6. *Client–server database architecture*

DBMS (database management systems) are software programs that manage databases. A DBMS supports the structuring, storage, updating and maintenance of a database. It is the only interface between computer scientists and data (definition of schemas, programming of applications), as well as between users and data (consultation and updating).

A DBMS must allow:

– data to be described independently of applications;

– data to be manipulated: data to be queried and updated without specifying an access algorithm;

– data to be controlled: integrity, confidentiality (control of access rights);

– data to be shared: a database is shared between several users and applications at the same time, so it is necessary to be able to control concurrent access;

– data to be secure: recovery after failure, logging of events;

– ensured data access performance;

– physical independence: being able to modify storage structures or indexes without any repercussions at the application level;

– logical independence: allowing different applications to have different views of the same data.

A DBMS is in charge of a lot of tasks!

4.5.2. DBMS models

There are three main DBMS models, differentiated according to the representation of the data contained in the database.

4.5.2.1. The hierarchical model

The data is classified hierarchically, in a top-down tree structure. This model uses pointers between the different records. This is the first generation of DBMS, which appeared in the 1970s.

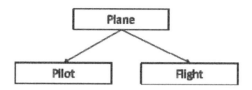

Figure 4.7. *Example of a hierarchical diagram*

4.5.2.2. *The relational model*

The early work on DBs is generally attributed to Ted Codd (1970), an IBM researcher. In this model, data are stored in two-dimensional tables (rows and columns) called relations. The data are manipulated by relational algebra operators such as intersection, join, or Cartesian product. This is the second generation of DBMS (1980s).

Students			Units of study			Registrations		
172	Dupont		1	DB		172	1	2016
173	Durand		2	OS		172	2	2017
174	Martin					173	1	2015
						174	2	2017

Figure 4.8. *Example of a relation*

Relational databases are the most widespread databases. The most used relational DBMS are Oracle, MySQL, Microsoft SQL Server, PostgreSQL and DB2.

4.5.2.3. *The object model*

The data are stored as objects, that is, structures called classes. Object databases make sense when it comes to modeling very rich and complex data with many variations: multimedia documents, geographical data, etc. This is the third generation (1990s). But the complexity of their implementation and the place already taken by RDBMS have severely limited the deployment of ODBMS.

4.5.3. *Database design*

Designing and setting up a database is a major task that can take weeks or even months, depending on the size of the database, before the data are even entered into the database. The work of analyzing the needs of the organization and the users involved is essential because it supports the overall success of the operation. Figure 4.9 summarizes the main steps.

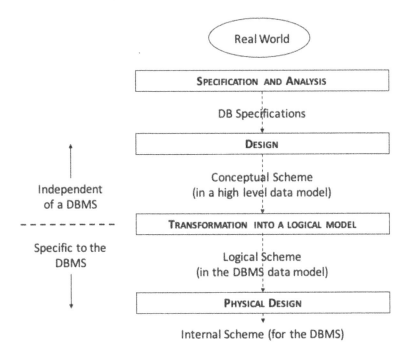

Figure 4.9. *Steps in database design*

4.5.4. *Enterprise resource planning (ERP) systems*

For a long time, companies and other organizations have set up several databases, each concerning one of the major functions: personnel, financial management, production and stock, customers, etc. However, these different databases contained some common data and it was difficult to ensure consistency. It was necessary to have a global vision of the organization's data in order to manage it efficiently.

The concept of an information management system (IMS) appeared in the mid-1960s in the United States and a few years later in France. However, this concept has evolved considerably up to the present day. Information management systems are influenced by research into system structures and the conceptualization of decision support at the IT level.

ERP (Enterprise Resource Planning) is a subset of information management systems. An ERP is a software solution aimed at unifying a company's information system by integrating the various functional components around a single database. Entering or modifying data in any of the modules (human resources, sales management, inventory management, production, etc.) impacts all the other modules: the database is updated and applies the change to the entire company.

An ERP meets specific characteristics:

– it emanates from a unique designer;

– in case of the impact of a module, the information is updated in real time in all the other associated modules;

– it is a system that guarantees the possibility of audit: it is easy to find and analyze the origin of each piece of information;

– it can cover the company's entire information system (unless the company chooses, in the first instance, to implement only certain modules of the ERP);

– it guarantees the uniqueness of the information it contains since it has only one database in the logical sense.

More than a simple piece of software, an ERP is a real project requiring a total integration of a software tool within an organization, and therefore has significant engineering costs. However, its implementation leads to significant changes in the work habits of a large number of staff. The organization concerned therefore often calls upon a specialized consulting firm.

4.5.5. *Other types of databases*

We especially mentioned the databases dedicated to the management of companies, administrations and other organizations, large or medium.

However, a large number of organizations have developed and are still developing the databases necessary for an efficient management and use of the information for which they are responsible. Here are a few examples.

4.5.5.1. *Knowledge bases*

The purpose of a knowledge base is to model and store a set of knowledge, ideas, concepts or data in a computerized manner and to allow their consultation/use.

Bringing together all documents, instructions, business processes and other elements in one place, the business knowledge base can be accessed and used by all employees at any time. These databases can be set up by companies to improve their internal operations and/or their relations with their customers, by various organizations to improve the relationship with their users, etc.

They are often associated with an expert system that will allow the user to use them: the user simply enters the information at his or her disposal, and the expert system gives him or her the answer. Troubleshooting is a fairly classic example of an application.

Some chatbots, or conversational agents, have a knowledge base in which all the information they need to answer users' questions is recorded.

4.5.5.2. *Geographic information systems*

A geographic information system (GIS) is an information system designed to collect, store, process, analyze, manage and present all types of spatial and geographic data. GIS offers all the possibilities of databases (such as querying and statistical analysis) through the unique visualization and geographic analysis specific to maps.

Many fields are closely related to geography: environment, demography, public health, territorial organization, network management, civil protection, etc. They have a direct interest in the power of GIS to create maps, to integrate all types of information, to better visualize various scenarios, to better present ideas and to better understand the scope of possible solutions.

There are two types of data in a GIS:

– data enabling the user to know the shape and the location in space of the observed geographical objects (essentially images composed of pixels);

– alphanumeric data enabling the user to describe geographical objects, to know their qualitative and/or quantitative characteristics.

For example, the CARTO database of the French IGN (*Institut géographique national*) contains a homogeneous vector description of the different elements of the country with decametric precision. It also offers a wealth of thematic information: road (more than 1 million km of roads) and rail networks, administrative units, hydrographic network, land use, etc.

Today, GIS represents a market worth several billion euros worldwide and employs several hundred thousand people.

4.5.5.3. Scientific databases

There are a large number of scientific databases in various fields. Here are three examples.

The *base de données publique des medicaments* (BDPM), the French public drug database, was opened in 2013. This administrative and scientific database on the treatment and proper use of health products is implemented by the *Agence nationale de sécurité du medicament et des produits de santé* (ANSM). It is intended for healthcare professionals, as well as for the general public.

SIMBAD (Set of Identifications, Measurements and Bibliography for Astronomical Data) is an astronomical database of objects outside the solar system. Created in 1980, it is maintained by the *Centre de données astronomiques* in Strasbourg and allows astronomers around the world to easily know the properties of each of the objects listed in an astronomical catalog. As of February 2017, SIMBAD contains more than 9 million objects with 24 million different names, and more than 327,000 bibliographical references have been entered.

The ***Observatoire Transmedia*** is a research platform that enables the analysis of large volumes of transmedia data (TV, radio, Web, AFP, Twitter) that are multimodal, heterogeneous and related to French and Francophone news. The consortium of this project led by the Ina (*Institut national de* *l'audiovisuel*) has brought together technological partners as well as partners in the human and social sciences, and has enabled the acquisition of know-how and tools for mass media processing. This platform has been renamed OTMedia+.

4.5.6. *Data protection in a database*

The importance of safety was emphasized in Chapter 2 of this work. Attacks coming from outside (networks) are not the only attacks, and the protection of data in a database must also take into account the problems, accidental or malicious, that may occur.

The fundamental principles are as follows:

– identification/authentication: who connects (access keys)?

– authorization: can you do this operation on this object?

– integrity: data must be protected against accidental or malicious modification;

– confidentiality: define the data that cannot be seen by unauthorized users;

– availability: systems must remain available to legitimate users;

– audit: continuous auditing and recording (logging) of the operations performed on the database is essential to resolve any security issues that may arise;

– restoration capability: the ability to reconstruct the database from backups and logs in the event of a serious incident.

And all other risks must be analyzed according to the specific context. For example, when an employee leaves the company, we have to make sure that his or her access rights to the database are removed.

4.6. Intelligence and Big Data

Here we are in the ultimate level of data, which combines intelligence with data.

Anything and everything can emit data: web browsing, e-mails, SMS, phone conversations, GPS, radios, bank cards, sensors, satellites, connected objects, etc. These data can be recorded for reuse after (or not). The volume of stored data is estimated in zettabytes (trillions of bytes) in 2020.

Unlike an organization's data, which are structured and can be stored in a database, there are a wide variety of formats (digital data, text, images, sound, video, etc.) and each has a low density of information. It is mainly a flow of data, like a fountain that flows continuously and from which we would take only a small part for our use.

All these data are stored and made available in huge storage spaces, the data centers introduced in Chapter 1.

Big Data refers to a very voluminous set of data that no conventional database management or data management tool can handle. Traditional computing, including business intelligence, **is model-based**; Big Data is about mathematics **finding patterns in data**.

Big Data is characterized by "3 Vs": its unprecedented **Volume**; its **Velocity**, which represents the frequency at which data are simultaneously generated, captured, shared and updated; its **Variety**: data are raw, semi-structured or even unstructured, coming from multiple sources.

Data only makes sense with the algorithms that process them. To process this phenomenal amount of data, two types of means must be combined: very powerful computers and efficient algorithms capable of extracting useful information.

In **data mining** applications, raw information is collected and placed in a giant database, then analyzed and summarized to extract potentially useful information. Data mining is at the crossroads of several scientific and technological fields (machine learning, pattern recognition, databases, statistics, artificial intelligence, data analysis, data visualization, etc.), which are presented in Figure 4.10.

Data mining is part of the Knowledge Discovery in Databases (KDD) process, which is summarized in Figure 4.11.

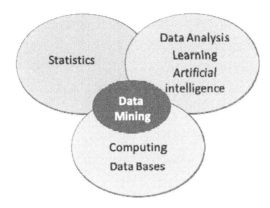

Figure 4.10. *Position of data mining. For a color version of this figure, see www.iste.co.uk/delhaye/computing.zip*

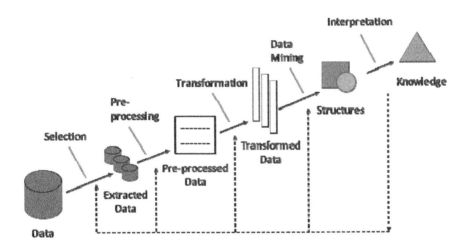

Figure 4.11. *Knowledge extraction. For a color version of this figure, see www.iste.co.uk/delhaye/computing.zip*

Data mining applications are used in many areas, including:

– commercial marketing and e-commerce: personalized product recommendation, customer follow-up (analysis of customer loyalty and customer loss), competitive price analysis;

– risk/fraud management: detection of fraud (credit card fraud, counterfeiting, etc.);

– the environment: climatic simulations, atmospheric pollution, the fight against deforestation, etc.;

– security and fight against crime, detection of threats;

– health: identification of disease risk factors, detection and monitoring of epidemics, pharmacovigilance, etc.;

– industry: predictive maintenance, logistics, etc.;

– politics: analysis of the political opinions of the population.

The use of these vast amounts of data can be worrisome, and several types of risks to privacy and fundamental rights have been reported in the literature:

– dehumanization: most individuals can feel dehumanized, that is, they can no longer protect the data that concerns them and that is collected, analyzed and sold without their knowledge;

– the possibility of deleting data relating to a natural person on simple request of the latter (right to oblivion);

– undue inferences, misinterpretation of certain data;

– exacerbating the digital divide, as data mining tools provide a few companies with increasing and almost instant access to billions of digitized data and documents;

– monopolistic appropriation of certain Big Data sets collected by a few large companies (Google, Facebook) or by the public or secret tools of certain States;

– ethically unsustainable abuses, including in social networks that collect a large amount of data and information about their users and the networks they join.

Data mining is one of the new research and development priorities of many organizations, companies, universities, research centers, etc. According to IDC (International Data Corporation), the Big Data market is expected to reach $203 billion in revenue in 2020, compared to $130 billion in 2016. That is how significant this field is becoming in the global economy!

4.7. Data ownership and Open Data

This deluge of digital data poses a number of problems, including its quality and the legal possibility of using it. Do I have the right to use, for commercial purposes in particular, any data I find on the Web? Does its use not infringe on a legal right?

Let us recall that intellectual property is the domain comprising all the exclusive rights granted on intellectual creations. It comprises two branches: literary and artistic property, which applies to works of the mind (copyright), and industrial property, which mainly concerns patents.

Data ownership has been the subject of legal debate for years and is approached in different ways in different countries. In France, as in many countries, the notion of data ownership has no legal status as such.

No intellectual property rights are generally attached to raw data (my date of birth, for example). On the contrary, someone who takes a picture of me on a Brazilian beach without my knowledge has no right to publish it without my agreement, even if I am not a movie star! That is the right to the image.

More seriously, the images acquired by the SPOT satellite constellation constitute a cost-effective source of information, suitable for the knowledge, monitoring, forecasting and management of resources and human activities on our planet. They have a significant value and are therefore protected and commercialized.

Things continue to get more complicated, for example, with the connected objects already mentioned: Should the property rights on captured data be assigned to the manufacturers of connected objects, or to those who use these connected objects to capture data?

The debates, which concern more than lawyers alone, will undoubtedly continue for many years to come.

4.7.1. *Personal data*

Our personal data is captured by GAFA (e-mails, cell phones, social networks, Internet browsing, shopping carts, etc.) and many others, no doubt.

The data concerning our tastes, our travels or our loves, are broken down, collected, aggregated, and often resold.

In addition, they are used for a variety of purposes: commercial (I experience it every day, like everyone else, especially when I surf the Web and receive advertising pop-ups), political (the recent scandal surrounding the Cambridge Analytica company is just one example), all kinds of proselytism, etc. And nobody asks me if I agree!

Our personal data are subject to a fundamental right, the right to privacy. Each individual should be able to freely decide on the use of the data that concern him or her. This is not the case because the legal vagueness is great and no one is going to attack a Web giant for using his or her personal data in an analysis involving enormous amounts of data. The question for the individual is therefore not so much one of ownership of his or her data as it is of keeping control of the data flows concerning him or her.

However, in 2018, we witnessed debates aimed at allowing each person to monetize his or her personal data, which currently enriches the giants of the Internet. Is this realistic and even useful?

But better regulation is needed, and the European Union's General Data Protection Regulation (GDPR)[1], which is the reference text for personal data protection, came into force in 2018. The main objectives of the GDPR are to increase both the protection of persons concerned by the processing of their personal data and the accountability of those involved in such processing.

This text integrates the right to erasure for any person in Article 17, which states that the person "has the right to obtain from the data controller the erasure of personal data concerning him/her without undue delay, and the controller shall have the obligation to erase personal data without undue delay"; this is what is called the right to digital oblivion.

4.7.2. Opening up public data: Open Data

Open Data refers to a (worldwide) movement to open up data to meet the growing need of economic, academic and cultural players to collect and analyze masses of data. Open Data is digital data that is freely accessible and

---

1 https://www.cnil.fr/en/general-data-protection-regulation-guide-assist-processors.

usable. It can be of public or private origin, produced in particular by a community, a public service or a company. It is disseminated in a structured manner according to a method and an open license guaranteeing its free access and reuse by all without technical, legal or financial restrictions.

Since 2003, the European Union has been working on this subject and has produced several directives. On April 25, 2018, the European Commission adopted a proposal to revise the Public Sector Information (PSI) Directive, including various measures to create a European data space. The reuse of Open Data has an important interest in addressing societal challenges for the development of new technologies, etc. The reuse of Open Data is of great interest in the approach of societal challenges, for the development of new technologies, etc. The reuse of Open Data is a key element in the development of a European Data Area.

The European Data Portal[2] collects metadata of public sector information available on the public data portals of the different European countries. In addition, the European Union Open Data Portal[3] provides access to Open Data published by EU institutions and bodies.

In France, the Etalab mission[4] coordinates the policy of opening up and sharing public data. It develops and runs the Open Data[5] platform, which is designed to collect and make freely available all the public information held by the State, its public institutions and, if they so wish, local authorities and public or private sector bodies responsible for public service missions.

---

2 www.europeandataportal.eu.

3 www.data.europa.eu.

4 www.etalab.gouv.fr.

5 www.data.gouv.fr.

5

Technology Building Blocks

It is important to understand the main technological trends that allow us to build the services we have today and that profoundly change our daily lives. We will detail some applications and uses in Chapter 6, as they often combine several of these technologies.

5.1. Embedded systems

The explosion of the Internet of Things (IoT) gave a special importance to the technology of embedded systems, which are autonomous electronic and computer systems dedicated to a specific task, often in real time, with a limited size and low energy consumption. They are called embedded systems because they are generally not seen. It is therefore not a traditional computer that can be used for many applications.

It is often a component of a larger system. It interacts with the external environment by retrieving information via sensors and acting on this environment via actuators to produce an action. We are in a scheme of "information ↔ reaction". Embedded systems are numerous in transportation (automotive, aviation, etc.), electrical and electronic products (digital watches, telephony, television, washing machines, home automation, etc.), telecommunications, medical equipment, process control (production lines, etc.), smart cards, consumer toys, etc.

The characteristics of an embedded system can be summarized as follows:

– it is generally built to perform a single task or function, although more generalized embedded systems are developing;

– it must comply with certain constraints: small size, performance, reliability, cost;

– it must be able to react continuously, within often specified time frames, to changes in its environment (we discussed real time in Chapter 3);

– it has one (or more) microprocessor(s) or microcontroller(s);

– it has an internal memory (ROM) to store its software;

– it has input/output ports to communicate with the outside world;

– it must be robust and reliable in many cases, both in terms of hardware and software, because its operation may concern the safety of people and property, security, the accomplishment of missions;

– its energy consumption can be constrained to have a maximum autonomy.

The importance of these criteria varies from one area of use to another.

5.1.1. *Specific architectures*

Like any computer system, an embedded system is organized into three levels as described at the beginning of Chapter 3: hardware, operating system and application.

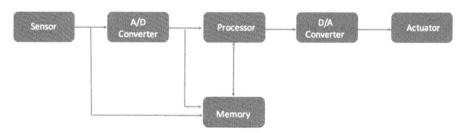

Figure 5.1. *Basic architecture of an embedded system*

The hardware level consists, in most cases, of one or more microprocessor(s) and microcontroller(s), integrated on a chip with memory, and input–output ports often with converters to switch from the analog to the digital world and vice versa. A simple system can be satisfied with an 8- or 16-bit microcontroller, but processors can be very complex in some systems, to the point of having massively parallel architectures. More than 90% of the processors manufactured worldwide are for embedded systems, so this is a huge market.

The operating system should be as small as possible and highly reliable. Several examples of operating systems are given in Chapter 3.

The application must obey the same constraints: efficiency, reliability and compactness. Its development is closely linked to these constraints, the hardware and the operating system.

The design of an embedded system often uses co-design techniques, enabling the hardware and software to be designed for a functionality to be implemented. The steps are the specification (list of system functionalities in an abstract way), hardware and software modeling, partitioning (hardware/software), synthesis of hardware and software (leading to a system-on-chip), and testing.

Training courses exist to strengthen expertise in engineering connected objects, critical embedded real-time systems, security, joint software/ hardware design and modeling of complex systems.

5.1.2. *Some fields of use*

The impressive growth in the number of connected objects (more than 80 billion in 2020, according to various sources) shows that the embedded systems industry is constantly producing new techniques and opportunities. They can be found in transportation, homes and offices, health, communicating objects (starting with our telephones), the industry, etc. Here is an overview of their place in a few areas; they will be found in Chapter 6.

5.1.2.1. *Transportation*

All means of transport use embedded systems: planes, cars, trains, subways and even electric scooters. We will talk about cars in Chapter 6 and will simply mention avionics here.

Avionics covers techniques related to the electrical equipment, electronics and computer equipment used to fly an aircraft. Embedded systems have radically changed the way an aircraft is piloted: the pilot no longer directly controls the separate elements of the aircraft (engines, ailerons, flaps), but controls the aircraft at a higher level of abstraction. According to its function, each of these computers interacts with a certain number of sensors and actuators, by means of electronic circuits for acquisition and specific commands.

The latest generation of aircraft, recently represented by the Airbus A350, has led to an accelerated increase in the number of application functions to be embedded: flight management, fuel management, anti-collision system, ground proximity warning, equipment monitoring to improve maintenance, cabin environment management, etc. There are now more than 100 computers and software representing tens of millions of lines of code in a modern aircraft.

The importance of software and sensors in airliners may raise questions. The two Boeing 737 MAX crashes in October 2018 and March 2019 involved the MCAS stall protection system and highlighted shortcomings in the development and verification of MCAS software. Humans, in this case the pilot, must be able to regain control of the machine.

5.1.2.2. *Home automation*

Household appliances have long been equipped with embedded systems: washing machines, induction hobs, refrigerators, etc. Home automation increasingly integrates connected objects, most often using wireless protocols such as ZigBee, Bluetooth or Wi-Fi. In the kitchen, appliances are able to make the different elements (hob and hood, for example) talk to each other. We can imagine a refrigerator knowing what it contains and alerting us that there is no more milk!

The living room is the preferred space for multimedia: TV, connected speakers, games consoles, wall-mounted video projectors, voice assistants, etc. Automatic openings and closings (gate, garage door, shutters, blinds) are increasingly manageable remotely. We can control security cameras and receive images from our phone.

With connected lighting, the dream of controlling all your light bulbs by voice or from your smartphone and tablet becomes a reality. Light bulb Wi-Fi or Bluetooth: there is nothing like it to create a lighting ambience adapted to everyday life.

Energy management is also an interesting sector, especially if several energy sources are used (photovoltaic, heat pump, gas, etc.). We can optimize our consumption and energy needs for heating, air-conditioning, domestic hot water and lighting.

And there are, and will be, many other applications, especially with the objects we wear: phones with their multiple services, watches that record our heartbeat, etc.

5.1.2.3. *Infrastructure monitoring*

The maintenance of infrastructure such as large networks or engineering structures such as bridges and dams requires regular monitoring work, the cost of which represents a high fraction of the maintenance budget. It is a matter of coping with wear and aging and planning maintenance in the best possible conditions. Bridges are subject to vehicle traffic and climatic actions (frost, heat, wind, etc.). They are monitored, in particular thanks to sensor networks, according to precise procedures to ensure their maintenance, prevent and diagnose possible problems, as well as ensure their maintenance and the necessary repairs.

The monitoring and maintenance of offshore infrastructures involves the use of numerous sensors (pressure, vibration, corrosion, etc.) necessary to monitor their operating condition and wear and tear.

The French rail network SNCF deploys sensors on infrastructures, catenaries and rails: data are collected in real time and processed to warn maintenance departments and even anticipate possible operations to be carried out on the network, which does not prevent us from experiencing delays due to various causes.

The industry makes massive use of embedded systems for process control, through production robotics, as well as to monitor possible anomalies and to secure the working environment of the personnel, for energy management, security (intrusion alert), etc. Industrial sites with major accident risks, known as Seveso sites, are of course particularly concerned.

5.2. Artificial intelligence (AI)

5.2.1. *A bit of history*

What is called artificial intelligence has an increasingly important role in various applications. In recent years, it has been of interest to many scientific and economic players and has made the headlines.

This is a subject that has long interested me since I was one of the first students to complete a PhD in this field. It was in 1969 at the Faculty of Sciences in Paris. I was interested in the automatic demonstration of mathematical theorems, while others focused on games such as chess. The idea was to show that it was possible to design algorithms and write software that would allow a computer to find solutions in activities considered to be specific to human intelligence.

At that time, it was a real challenge to show that a computer could play chess correctly, that is, by respecting its rules. Since then, the performance of computers and the progress of research, especially in learning, have reached such a level that a computer can beat the best players.

The Larousse encyclopedia defines AI as "a set of theories and techniques implemented to create machines capable of simulating human intelligence." We will see that this definition is too restrictive. The notion of AI was born in the 1950s thanks to the mathematician Alan Turing, already quoted in Chapter 1 of this book. In his book *Computing Machinery and Intelligence*, he raises the question of bringing a form of intelligence to machines. But this raises another question: is there a quantifiable definition of intelligence? Creativity and consciousness are part of intelligence! For John McCarthy[1], "all intellectual activity can be described with sufficient precision to be simulated by a machine," which restricts the notion of

---

1 John McCarthy (1927–2011) was the main pioneer of artificial intelligence with Marvin Lee Minsky. He received a PhD in mathematics from Princeton University in 1951. From 1962 until his retirement in 2000, McCarthy was a professor at Stanford University. He received the Turing Prize in 1971 for his work in artificial intelligence.

intelligence. This discipline is therefore at the crossroads of computer science, electronics and cognitive science.

Until the mid-1970s, work on AI was plentiful (research on machine translation, robotics, vision, etc.) and produced some results. But AI was soon to fall victim to its original promises that were not kept despite significant funding, from the American agency DARPA in particular. AI survived its first winter in the mid-1970s.

With the advent of expert systems (programs that answer questions in a given field of knowledge, using logical rules derived from the knowledge of human experts in that field) and the approach of machine learning algorithms that allow computers to train on data sets and use statistical analysis to produce values, AI got a second wind until the end of the 1990s when, once again, everything came to a standstill, for much the same reasons: the results did not live up to expectations. This was the second winter.

It was in the mid-1990s that AI regained an important place thanks to the Internet, the massive amount of data it provides, and the increasing performance of computers. In 1997, the victory of IBM's Deep Blue computer against Gary Kasparov, world chess champion, popularized the idea that a computer can be smart even though the Deep Blue program was just a set of rules, having a huge memory capacity where thousands of chess games were stored along with the different paths to victory.

We then witnessed a commercial recovery of AI, which became a marketing argument. There are many examples: "a robot vacuum cleaner that is able to clean a room by itself" (course material from a French school); "intelligent washing machine: this intelligent technology detects the laundry load and automatically adjusts the washing settings, to guarantee you perfect results" (advertisement from a major brand). Where is the intelligence? In September 2019, a Google AI manager described an example: a computer is given 2,000 images of clouds associated with the cloud type (cirrus, cumulus, etc.), and then presented with a new image to find the cloud type; the answer is not linked to any intelligence, but to algorithms that compare two images and calculate a similarity rate.

5.2.2. *Intelligence or statistics?*

If I use the recipe as an example of the algorithm mentioned in Chapter 1, everything goes well if I have all the ingredients indicated in the recipe. But it turns out that my grocer does not have the chervil that is part of this list. What should I replace it with? My idea is to replace the chervil with flat parsley. I think this is the best solution; it is a "heuristic" because it is not an absolute guarantee and another person may make another choice.

In chess, I have the choice between several moves; for each of them my opponent has several choices of reply, and so on. I cannot imagine all the possible moves when I continue this analysis, which results in a tree structure that very quickly becomes extremely complex. At some point, I will have to make a choice that I feel is the best possible based on my experience. It may not be the best choice, but I base my choice on "heuristics", which is different from chance because my choice is based on experience gained from many games. As such, we are in the field of statistics.

The example of the recipe is simple; the second example is less simple because it requires planning. And some tasks, such as translating a text or conducting dialogue, are much more complicated because they require a lot of knowledge, experience and common sense.

Can we develop algorithms that allow machines to solve these types of problems? What is called AI today is the realization of algorithms enabling the extraction of a property or a piece of information from successive experiments on large quantities of data (Big Data). AI has come out of its second winter thanks to the progress made in learning that is associated with intelligence.

5.2.3. *Important work around automatic learning*

AI is based on an ambitious goal: to understand how human cognition works and to reproduce it; to create cognitive processes comparable to those of humans. Our knowledge is the result of complex learning processes that take place throughout our lives. Can computers learn? The answer is yes. Can they invent, like humans? The answer is no.

This is a far cry from the general approach of AI capable of solving a wide variety of problems, adapting and learning; but AI specialized for a specific class of problems is much more promising and therefore focuses the bulk of research efforts.

It is the progress of machine learning methods that has allowed AI to develop and find an important place in many fields. This is because we have more and more data and more and more powerful computers. We can distinguish two levels of learning that we are going to summarize: machine learning and deep learning.

Machine learning has been used for many years. Summarizing one example, it has consisted of providing the machine with thousands of different images of an object (an animal, a car, etc.) and telling it each time that it is a dog or a giraffe or a car, etc. The machine gradually adapts its parameters to be able to distinguish which type of object is on an image. This is a bit like the trial-and-error method (we learn little by little from our mistakes as well as from our successes). This applies to words, sounds, etc. This method is also called supervised learning.

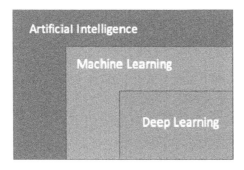

Figure 5.2. *Learning levels. For a color version of this figure, see www.iste.co.uk/delhaye/computing.zip*

The machine will then be able to correctly classify images of cars or dogs that it has never seen during the learning phase. But can we really talk about intelligence? A system has to analyze tens of thousands of images of dogs in order to recognize a dog in a collection of images with good precision, whereas a very young child can distinguish a cat from a dog.

In the 1990s, work on deep learning, using neural networks (highly simplified models of neurons in the human brain), gave a new perspective to AI research.

This learning and classification system, based on networks of artificial digital neurons, is composed of thousands of units (neurons) that each performs small simple calculations. Each neural network is composed of tens or even hundreds of layers of neurons, each receiving and interpreting the information from the previous layer. The results of the first layer of neurons will be used as input for the calculation of the others. For example, the system will learn to recognize letters before attacking words in a text. This layered operation is what makes this type of learning "deep".

It is this functioning that allowed the AlphaGo program, developed by Google, to beat the world champion of the game of Go, Ke Jie, on May 27, 2017. This victory was obtained after many training sessions with humans, with other computers and especially with itself.

5.2.4. A multiplication of applications

From the beginning of the 2010s, we have witnessed an explosion of work that has led to very diverse applications.

These so-called intelligent systems allow us to talk to our smartphones relatively naturally (Google Assistant or Siri, for example), ask them questions and listen to answers (more or less relevant) with increasingly realistic voices.

Image recognition is already widely used in many fields such as security, (semi-) autonomous cars, medical image analysis, automatic text translation (even if it is doubtful that an IT system can translate a poem by Louis Aragon better than professional translators), health (with predictive medicine, access to "virtual doctors" in remote areas) and automatic moderation of social networks. AI is being introduced into connected objects, whether they are intelligent vehicles, smart homes, smart cities, surveillance systems or drones and robots. There are many uses: characterization (gender, age, attributes) or identification of users in real time, and behavior analysis (emotion, fatigue, attention). For mass distribution, it can provide a tool for analyzing consumer behavior. On the stock market, algorithms become the first buyers of bonds, stocks and commodities. Is this really intelligence?

A big question is usually overlooked: can we trust the decision made by an AI-based system? It cannot be formally proven that AI provides safe results. This shows that trusting it blindly when the decision may have serious consequences (as in the case of autonomous cars, for example) is a gamble. But humans themselves do not always make the right decision!

In addition, we should not underestimate the ethical issues that AI can raise, especially because of the accumulation of data stored on individuals. The use of so-called predictive technologies in the field of law enforcement or justice raises the problem of individual liberties. My health insurance company could change the amount of my contribution based on predictions from an analysis of my profile. We must therefore be careful that the use of algorithms does not transform our choices of society.

5.2.5. *The challenges of AI*

The opportunities are such that AI, especially deep learning, is seen as one of the strategic technologies of the future. The few examples of applications mentioned above show this.

All the major Internet groups (Google, Facebook, Apple, IBM, Microsoft, etc.) have launched research programs with funding in the billions of euros, and have created start-ups targeting specific applications.

Several countries, including the United States, China, South Korea and Russia, have embarked on ambitious programs in this area.

The European Union strongly supports activities in the field of AI, with three priorities:

– strengthening the EU's scientific, technological and industrial base;

– preparing for socio-economic changes related to AI;

– ensuring an appropriate legal and ethical framework.

In France, on November 28, 2018, the government presented a national strategy for research in AI based on the report presented in the spring of

2018 by MP and mathematician Cédric Villani. Funded by the State to the tune of 665 million euros between now and 2022, this strategy aims to establish France sustainably in the top five countries that are experts in AI worldwide. Utopia? In any case, this strategy must be part of a European framework if we want to achieve critical mass in the face of the Americans and the Chinese.

5.2.6. *What about intelligence?*

Although much studied scientifically, there is no clear definition of intelligence, and many questions remain unanswered. But intelligence cannot be reduced to the ability to solve a specific problem, for example, beating the world chess champion. Real life requires making many more choices than playing chess. Goals are often vague and evaluation difficult. We must take into account the sensitive experience of the world and reject the idea of knowledge reduced to mind and reason.

AI has become much more efficient thanks to the development of learning theories and the tremendous growth in computer performance. Today's systems, no matter how powerful they are, are specialized: they can only do what they were created to do. They lack the ability to acquire new skills in any field, which is a characteristic of human intelligence. Our learning is unsupervised because it allows us to uncover and understand the world in all its dimensions.

The field of computer science inspired by the human brain is still in its infancy. Although deep learning has become a buzzword in less than three years, there is still much work to be done in this exciting field. Yann LeCun[2], one of the pioneers of deep learning, is pragmatic and reminds us that the AI field has often suffered from disproportionate expectations.

This notion of AI is the subject of many debates. Personalities such as Bill Gates, astrophysicist Stephen Hawking, and Tesla CEO Elon Musk expressed their concerns in 2015 about the progress made in the field of AI, which they considered potentially dangerous. But Bill Gates has since reportedly revised his position.

---

2 Yann Le Cun, a French researcher in artificial intelligence, was awarded the Turing Prize (considered the equivalent of the Nobel Prize in the field of computer science) in 2019. See his latest book (Le Cun 2019).

In reality, it is a set of technologies that become essential: they assist us in many tasks. They rely on increasingly sophisticated algorithms to provide an environment for developing services and applications to help us in decision-making. Luc Julia (2019) prefers to talk about "augmented intelligence" in his book *L'intelligence artificielle n'existe pas*, rejecting the idea that machines will be able to take power over humans.

Will the virtual human brain, the goal of projects such as the Brain Initiative in the United States or the Human Brain Project in Europe, be intelligent?

5.3. The Internet

Chapter 2 gave a brief presentation of the Internet, its history, the protocols used, etc. But the Internet has and will increasingly mark our personal environments and society as a whole. It is therefore an essential technological base.

The evolution of the Internet can be summarized in five phases. The first was the connection of two and then several computers. Then the Web allowed access to shared services. The possibility of connecting mobile devices marked a new stage, the mobile Internet. The arrival of social networks and the communication of groups of people was the fourth phase. Finally, the Internet of Things is the stage we are currently experiencing.

5.3.1. *Mobility*

Mobile Internet is the set of technologies designed to access the Internet using mobile networks, in particular the networks accessible by our phones. Its very rapid development has been possible thanks to the development of networks, on the one hand (3G, 4G and soon 5G), and terminal equipment, on the other hand.

Tablets, and especially smartphones, with high-definition screens, are repositioning computers to navigate the Web. Arcep (*Autorité de regulation des communications électroniques et des postes*, the French regulatory authority for electronic communications and postal services) indicated, in its 2018 edition of the "Baromètre du numérique", that 46% of French people over the age of 12 years use their smartphone to access the Internet.

After 3G networks, 4G networks (introduced in 2013) allowed mobile data to increase loading speed considerably. 4G allows web pages to be displayed almost instantaneously, to stream HD videos without any difficulty, etc.

We must not forget Wi-Fi technology, which makes it possible to avoid using the services of an operator. When American or Brazilian friends arrive at my house, they ask me for the password to my Wi-Fi box, which allows them to communicate with their country for free from their phone! In addition, Wi-Fi access points are multiplying in all public places. Websites are developing interfaces adapted to telephones, particularly in e-commerce.

5.3.2. *Social networks*

The Internet has witnessed the rise of social networks, some of which have become real social media, allowing Internet users and professionals to create a profile page and share information, photos and videos with their network. The mobile is omnipresent: more than five out of six users use their mobile phone to access social networks.

We can distinguish several categories of social networks: generalist networks (Facebook, Twitter, etc.), professional networks (LinkedIn, Viadeo, etc.), video networks (YouTube, Periscope, etc.), visual networks (Instagram, Pinterest, etc.), and community networks of all kinds. Facebook is the most active network with 2.3 billion users per month worldwide (35 million alone in France).

Online conversations allow us to understand the new democratic balances, as well as the consumption trends of millions of individuals. This is why specialized companies offer services that allow companies to take advantage of the power of social media. However, we can have the feeling that these platforms are useless when delirious emotional flows are pouring out where vulgarity, manipulation and aggressiveness between members can reign supreme. This being the case, they have been unavoidable platforms for several years, even if some countries, such as China, are trying to turn them around.

Dangers associated with social networks exist, such as:

– addiction: likes and requests from friends lead to spending more and more time in front of the screen; young people are particularly vulnerable;

– cyber-bullying or harassment: the media frequently report news stories, especially in schools, with sometimes dramatic outcomes;

– the misappropriation or theft of personal data communicated imprudently by Internet users.

5.3.3. *The Internet of Things*

This is the world in which objects are able to exchange information and communicate with each other, as well as to communicate and interact with their users using the Internet and also other less known but still efficient communication networks (see Chapter 2).

5.3.4. *The Cloud*

Also explained in Chapter 2, the Cloud allows us to store and access our data (such as our photos) on any computer or smartphone connected to the Internet, anywhere on the planet! But the protection and use of our data remains questionable.

5.3.5. *Blockchain*

Blockchain is a technology created in 2008 by an individual known as Satoshi Nakamoto, whom no one has ever seen, with Bitcoin (the much-talked about cryptocurrency) as its first application. Simply put, blockchain is a distributed database system that makes it possible to render forgery-proof transaction history. Blockchain is "a technology for storing and transmitting information that is transparent, secure and operates without a central control body" (definition of Blockchain France).

Blockchain allows a transfer of value (money or other) without an intermediary (bank or other). It allows data to be recorded that are authenticated, certified and cannot be repudiated.

There are public blockchains, open to all, and private blockchains, whose access and use are limited to a certain number of actors. The decentralized nature of the blockchain, coupled with its security and transparency, promises much broader applications than the monetary domain.

The Internet has a very important role in the implementation of this technology. One of the problems encountered is energy consumption because the "miners", who are responsible for validating transactions, use complex algorithms that involve many computers.

5.3.6. *Vulnerabilities*

We have discussed security in the different areas of IT technologies and applications, and will continue to do so in the remainder of this book. Vulnerability can have an impact that is not very serious, for example, in connected objects (although the impact could be serious if a hacker took control of your car!).

More generally, what would be the consequences of a coordinated attack on global banking networks or on government networks or those used by airlines? The military are of course very concerned and also use specific networks that are not connected to the Internet, while at the same time developing very advanced research in the field of security (*DGA Maîtrise de l'information*, located near Rennes, in France, is a very important research center in this field).

5.4. Image processing and vision

Image processing is a discipline of computer science and applied mathematics that studies digital images and their transformations, with the aim of improving their quality or extracting information from them. It began long before the appearance of digital photography, which we all know, since it gradually took the place of analog photography, born at the beginning of the 19th century, with electronic sensors (CCD or CMOS) replacing film.

It is a technology that we will find in a large number of applications.

5.4.1. *A bit of history*

Image processing began to be studied in the 1920s for the transmission of images via the submarine cable linking New York and London. The first image digitization with data compression reduced the transfer time from more than a week to less than three hours, but the first computers powerful enough to carry out image processing appeared in the 1960s.

Since the beginning of the conquest of space, more than 60 years ago, space imagery has changed our representations of the planet. Its instruments provide a multitude of useful information to meet the major scientific and socio-economic challenges of our time, including climate change.

While the image made its appearance in medicine with the discovery of X-rays by Wilhelm Röntgen in 1896, the computer processing of medical images developed from the end of the 1960s.

Since the 1970s, there has been a diversification in the use of images: geography, biology, astronomy, medicine, agronomy, nuclear, robotics, surveillance and security, industrial control, television, satellite, microscopy, multimedia, etc. This development is closely linked to the progress made by research in the fields of mathematics, computer science and electronics.

5.4.2. *Image sources and their uses*

We are used to images that represent visible scenes; these are the images of everyday life. But there are many sources of images, associated with physical phenomena and adapted sensors.

X-rays are one of the oldest sources of electromagnetic radiation used in imaging. They are used to locate pathologies (infections, tumors) using radiography or CT scans. They are also used in industry and astronomy. Ultraviolet, which is not visible, is used in the analysis of minerals, gems or for the identification of all kinds of things such as banknotes. Infrared is particularly used in remote sensing (geology, cartography, weather forecasting), microscopy, photography, etc. Radars use microwaves. Radio waves are used in medicine for magnetic resonance imaging or in astronomy. Ultrasound is used in the exploration of oil deposits, or to monitor a pregnancy (obstetrics).

Devices can combine several types of spectra, for example on Earth observation satellites that differentiate between soils, vegetation, snow and clouds, areas with different temperatures, etc.

5.4.3. *The digital image*

The computer representation of an image is necessarily discrete (made up of separate distinct values), whereas the image itself is continuous in nature ("smooth" variations); the digital image is represented by a set of numbers. It is thus necessary to digitize the analogical image in order to visualize it, print it, process it, store it on a data processing medium and transmit it on a network.

Digitization requires at the same time a discretization of space (**sampling**) and a discretization of intensities and colors (**quantification**).

Sampling (Figure 5.3) defines the spatial resolution of the image. A digital image is composed of a finite set of elements, called picture elements or pixels (in 3D, voxels). The more dots per inch (dpi), the better the resolution and therefore the quality of the image.

Each pixel is located by two x and y coordinates in the image frame. A 2D image is therefore an object represented by a two-dimensional array of elementary surfaces (the pixels).

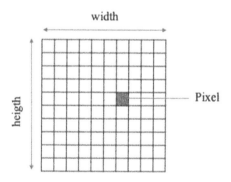

Figure 5.3. *Sampling an image*

A digital grayscale image is an array of integers between 0 and 255 (the value 0 corresponds to black, and the value 255 corresponds to white), which are therefore encoded on 8 bits (1 byte).

A color image is composed of three independent images to represent the three primary colors (red, green and blue). Each pixel of the color image thus contains three numbers (r, v, b), each being an integer between 0 and 255. We will thus have 24 bits per pixel.

Figure 5.4 shows three examples of displaying an image with different resolutions and therefore different qualities: 1,159 x 298 pixels, 800 x 206 pixels, 320 x 82 pixels.

Figure 5.4. *Three different resolutions (source: Wikimedia Commons). For a color version of this figure, see www.iste.co.uk/delhaye/computing.zip*

A video sequence (2D) is a dynamic scene with moving 2D objects. 2D video sequences are a juxtaposition of 2D images, where time is seen as a third dimension.

A volume image (3D) is an object represented by a three-dimensional array of elementary volumes (voxels). A volume can be seen as a stack of 2D images (e.g. scanner sections for 3D reconstruction). A 3D sequence is a dynamic scene with moving 3D objects.

5.4.4. *Image storage and compression*

We store the images as files. The information that will be stored is the width, height and pixel values. We will also be able to save the name of the author, date, acquisition conditions, etc.

The volume of these files is very large, which poses serious problems, especially when it comes to transmitting them. For example, a color image with dimensions (pixels) 800 x 600 will occupy 1.4 million bytes. The images will be compressed to reduce the amount of information needed to represent them, while minimizing the loss of information as much as possible. Several compression formats exist, and we encounter them in our common use of image-manipulating applications.

The main uncompressed image formats are BITMAP (no loss of quality, but large files) and TIFF (Tagged Image File Format, a format recognized by all operating systems, with large files).

The main lossy compressed image formats are JPEG (with several possible quality levels depending on the compression ratio) whose successor (JPEG 2000) provides a better quality image and GIF (Graphic Interchange Format).

The images in Figure 5.5 show the degradation of quality as a function of the JPEG compression rate, with the volume occupied by this image decreasing from 2.88 MB for the actual size to 38.66 KB (the degradation is particularly visible on the clown's nose).

Figure 5.5. *Quality loss and compression ratio (source: Jean-Loïc Delhaye). For a color version of this figure, see www.iste.co.uk/delhaye/computing.zip*

In addition, certain standards have been defined for specific areas. This is the case of DICOM, an international standard for the computerized management of medical imaging data.

5.4.5. *Computing and images*

Computers allow us, on the one hand, to process images (i.e. to act on the components of the image), and, on the other hand, to analyze the images (i.e. to extract information from them). All of this calls upon various scientific fields: signal processing, computer science, statistics, optics, electronics, information theory, etc.

5.4.5.1. *Image processing*

This is all about getting a new image with different characteristics. We can quote:

– restoration, which aims to compensate for damage (noise, blur, etc.) or defects due, for example, to the shooting or the sensor;

– enhancement, to increase the quality of the visual perception of the image (brightness, contrast, etc.);

– compression, as we have discussed, which provides an image that can be stored and transferred more efficiently at the cost of some degradation;

– the tattoo (or watermarking), which allows information to be added, visible or not, in the image;

– a large number of transformations such as merging images, special effects, adding or removing elements, image retouching with software such as Photoshop, etc.

5.4.5.2. *Image analysis*

The purpose of image analysis is to extract information from the image. Among the tools used are filtering, segmentation and contour extraction.

The final step is the semantic analysis of the image in order to give meaning to it. It uses techniques, such as AI algorithms, to interpret the image by locating, characterizing and recognizing objects and other elements in the scene.

5.4.6. **Some applications**

Image processing is used in many applications. Here are some of them (some of them will be detailed in Chapter 6):

– aerial and spatial imagery, with various objectives: monitoring, analysis of natural resources (deforestation, for example), meteorology, mapping, etc.;

– medicine: image analysis (cytology, tomography, ultrasound) that facilitates the work of doctors and telesurgery;

– the industry with robotic vision or for the control of the manufacturing and quality stages;

– sciences: interventions in confined environments (nuclear power plants, for example), astronomy, biology;

– numerical indexing of multimedia databases, which consists of characterizing the content of documents and the information they contain;

– the military field: surveillance, automatic guidance of vehicles, topography;

– smart cities: analysis of traffic, pollution, etc.;

– vehicles whose increasing range relies on environmental analysis to detect obstacles.

5.5. Conclusion

Algorithms and software are the basis of these technologies, which are found in many applications that we will see in Chapter 6 and that we use daily or that are hidden from us for various reasons (industrial competition, surveillance, defense secrecy, etc.).

These technologies are the subject of intensive research in public and private organizations and are not without consequences for the evolution of our societies; we will discuss them again in Chapter 7.

Some Areas of Application

The technological building blocks that we have just described can be found, in whole or in part, in the various fields of computer use. We have selected seven of them: robots, virtual reality (VR) and augmented reality (AR), health, the connected (and soon autonomous?) car, the smart city, smart mobility and the factory of the future.

6.1. Robots

This sentence of Aristotle (384–322 BCE) holds our attention: "For if each instrument could accomplish its own work, obeying or anticipating the will of others, like the status of Daedalus, or the tripods of Hephaestus, which, says the poet, 'of their own accord entered the assembly of the Gods'; if, in like manner, the shuttle would weave and the plectrum touch the lyre without a hand to guide them, chief workmen would not want servants, nor masters slaves" (Book I, Part IV)[1].

The word robot is a Czech word formed in regard to *robota* (hard work, drudgery) and was used in 1920 by the writer Karel Tchapek. From time immemorial, humans have sought to design tools capable of facilitating their activities. But they have also tried to create machines with capabilities resembling those of living beings. The history of robotics is part of the development of these two approaches.

---

1 https://socialsciences.mcmaster.ca/econ/ugcm/3ll3/aristotle/Politics.pdf.

6.1.1. *A bit of history*

There are three main stages in the development of robots.

6.1.1.1. *Automatons*

Without going back to Antiquity, let us see how automatons have multiplied and perfected over time.

The first animated clocks were created towards the end of the first millennium. They can still be seen today on certain bell towers, such as the astronomical clock in Strasbourg Cathedral, created in 1352: at the stroke of 12:30, the automatons shake, the apostles parade, a rooster crows and flaps its wings.

In 1781, Jacquard's loom, which we mentioned in Chapter 1, selected the needles of the loom on a precise geometrical pattern thanks to a string of punched cards. We already have an important improvement since we can change the pattern by changing the cards.

In 1805, Henri Maillardet built a spring automaton capable of making drawings. This idea of having paintings created by automatons was taken up again, including recently in the exhibition "Artists and Robots" in 2018 at the Grand Palais in Paris.

6.1.1.2. *Robots*

The ATILF (*Analyse et traitement informatique de la langue française*) research unit at the CNRS defines a robot as "a device performing, thanks to a microprocessor-based automatic control system, a precise task for which it has been designed in the industrial, scientific, military or domestic field". Robotics is therefore the set of sciences and techniques allowing the design and realization of robots.

Unlike automatons, robots are sensor-equipped systems capable of acting autonomously. They have sensory organs collecting information about their environment that will influence their activity; this activity is driven by increasingly sophisticated software.

They first appeared with the Industrial Revolution and then invaded many areas that we will cover shortly. From heavy industrial robotics to the medical or military field, via domestic robotics, machines are part of our daily lives.

6.1.1.3. *Robots with intelligence*

The vast majority of today's robots perform repetitive tasks without dynamic learning. The next step is to have a certain autonomy of the machine, in various environments, and adaptability to unforeseen situations, not only according to a pre-set program. These so-called intelligent devices are capable of collecting information extracted from their environment, the processing of which will influence their operation.

Research efforts focus on new fields of application with a stronger concern for improving the learning and intelligence capabilities of today's robots through sophisticated algorithms.

6.1.2. Fields of use regarding robots today

Robots are used in more and more fields, with constantly evolving characteristics: miniaturization, mobility, adaptability, working environment (land, sea, air), etc.

6.1.2.1. *Production robots*

The first robots appeared in the 1960s, but for a long time they were confined to industrial use (automotive, aerospace, etc.). They were essentially manipulative robots installed in closed spaces (cages). They have multiplied and become more complex; some factories are now increasingly robotized (we can say that our cars are largely built by robots).

There has also been an increase in the automatic management of warehouses and logistics centers, with the use of mobile carts. In October 2019, Amazon opened its first robotized distribution center in France, covering $152,000\,m^2$. On a smaller scale, pharmacies have a robot installed at the back of their premises that stores and delivers boxes of medicines directly to the pharmacy counter in its dispensary.

Some production sites also use robots to replace humans in hostile environment interventions, as is the case in the nuclear industry.

The representation of the environment is an essential aspect in mobility, and the information from the various sensors (radar, cameras, tactile sensors, etc.) must be interpreted in the best possible way. Location and navigation strategies, allowing a mobile robot to move to reach a goal, are extremely diverse and account must be taken of possible unforeseen elements such as moving obstructions. Learning is part of the research related to mobile robotics.

Figure 6.1. *Assembly of welded sub-assemblies by robotization (source: Cité des sciences et de l'industrie). For a color version of this figure, see www.iste.co.uk/delhaye/computing.zip*

6.1.2.2. *Service robots*

Today, a large number of the developments concern the field of service robotics. A service robot operates autonomously, or semi-autonomously, to provide services useful for the well-being of humans or the proper functioning of equipment, excluding manufacturing operations. Although it still seems far away, the prospect of the massive arrival of robots in our daily lives is no longer science fiction.

Domestic robots intended for the general public made their appearance at the beginning of the 21st century, with, for example, vacuum cleaners (beginning in 2002 with the Roomba robot from the company iRobot). They are multiplying, especially in the field of leisure (toys, companion robots, etc.).

Another sector of service robotics is set to experience strong growth in the coming years: medical robots and more broadly all those robots for assisting medical personnel as well as the elderly or disabled (automated wheelchairs, motor assistance robots, etc.).

Delivery robots appear, and distribution giants prepare them. In some healthcare facilities, a robot is used to transport medications from the central pharmacy to the appropriate departments. Our favorite pizza may soon be delivered to us by a drone.

Finally, in addition to the complexity of tasks and environments, there is an essential factor in service robotics when operating in the presence of humans: how can we guarantee total safety for humans when robots are in their homes?

6.1.2.3. *Humanoid robots*

We have mentioned many types of robots, each of which is intended to perform more or less complex tasks and to replace, or at least help, the human hand in the execution of these tasks. But there is a considerable distance between the capabilities of these robots, even very sophisticated ones, and human capabilities. The dream of roboticists is to be able to create robots "in the image of humans".

Roboticists would like their robot to have the motor skills of humans because they are essential in many applications. Industry needs robots that can kneel or bend like a human, move around by resting not only on their feet, but also on their knees, hands or elbows, just as we do when we crawl.

Humanoid robotics faces a huge challenge: it is a question of getting as close as possible to the capacities of a complex living being, their motor abilities, as well as their social capacities and, ultimately, their cognitive capacities. Human appearance, which is what is put forward for publicity reasons, is neither the most important nor the most complicated point for roboticists.

There are many jobs in representation, in which appearance counts a lot, and we prefer that the robot that welcomes us looks like a human rather than an assembly of metal parts. This is true, for example, of the hotel receptionist who must be welcoming, the TV news presenter or the guide in a museum. Appearance, the quality of communication and the ability to express emotions all become important criteria.

Cognitive abilities are by far the most complex. Today, we can tell the robot to "go get a bottle of water from the fridge"; tomorrow, we can tell it to "make me lunch". We will be able to endow robots with a certain intelligence (learning, ability to adapt to the unexpected), but we will still be very far from a robot capable of feeling, opinion, creativity, living in a community, etc. (see section 5.2).

The main obstacle to the widespread use of these robots will not be technological or economic but social. These robots will have to be able to express emotions and react in a way close to that of a real human to be accepted in our daily life.

In addition to technical questions (locomotion, relationship with humans, intelligence, appearance, autonomy, ability to adapt to the unexpected, etc.), there are also philosophical questions (can humans accept being accompanied by robots that resembles them? Does a humanoid have the same responsibility as a human)?

6.1.2.4. Cobotics

Jobs and skills will continue to evolve, but the human element will always be present. Cobotics (a neologism derived from the words "cooperation" and "robotics"), or collaborative robotics, aims to develop robotic technologies in continuous interaction with humans. The robot is no longer intended to replace a human, but to help him/her, to assist him/her. The human remains focused on the most complex part of the task requiring dexterity, perception, analysis, learning and experience. Thus, a cobot is a robotic device designed, manufactured and used to interact with a human operator.

The fields of application in regard to cobotics are varied, since it is very present in industry, but it is also an important perspective in the fields of health (surgery, rehabilitation, assistance and substitution), home automation, the military field or for training.

Research focuses on the safety and efficiency of human–robot interaction (HRI) and on new cobot architectures, from stress amplification systems that provide power and endurance in human gestures to exoskeletons (articulated and motorized equipment attached to the body via the legs and pelvis, or even on the shoulders and arms, to facilitate movement by adding the force of electric motors).

6.1.3. *Communication in the world of robots*

Robots were first designed to operate in environments where all parameters were precisely controlled, which was the case in an assembly line in the automotive industry. These systems were unable to cope with changes in task and environment structure without reconfiguration or reprogramming. Today, robots can evolve in dynamic spaces in which they interact with other robots and humans.

The question of communication arises, just as it arises between humans in everyday life. If I do not know the language of my interlocutors, if I am visually (or hearing) impaired, my ability to interact is more limited, unless *ad hoc* devices can compensate for this disability.

Let us take the example of cobots or, more generally, industrial robots when communication with humans is essential. What are the main modalities of an HRI?

– physical means: this is the simplest interface, the operator manipulates the robot directly, or remotely, by means of a button, a wheel, a joystick, etc. This manipulation modifies the robot's action in the desired direction;

– remote control by means of a tablet or any other device enables sending the instructions to the robot;

– motion capture: the operator, equipped with a suitable device, can use movements to indicate to the robot what it must do;

– visual means: the operator has screens, virtual or AR systems, to obtain information on the task, on the state of the robot or on the environment in which it evolves;

– sound means, allowing the robot and the operator to communicate by means of predefined sounds, by means of a richer, even normal, language thanks to the technologies of recognition and vocal synthesis which are developing;

– brain-computer interfaces (BCIs) are developed in research laboratories. This involves using signals from the brain, for example, by being equipped with a device for electroencephalograms, to send commands to a robot. Science-fiction? We will see!

Environments linking several robots and several humans exist (warehouses, etc.) and will multiply. Communication will be even more complex.

6.1.4. *Fear of robots*

The development of robots and their ability to replace us in certain tasks can worry us.

A primary concern is that robotization would create fewer jobs than it would destroy. The OECD (Organisation for Economic Co-operation and Development) predicted in a May 2019 report that robotization is expected to reduce employment by 14% over the next 20 years. But many studies tend to show that job creation compensates, at least partially, for the jobs destroyed and that the jobs created are better qualified and better paid (which cannot satisfy those who have lost their jobs).

In several countries, automation technologies are seen as a solution to population decline. This is the case in Japan, and also in Germany where an annual net immigration of 400,000 people would be needed over the next two decades to compensate for the natural decline of the working-age population. Even if automation and AI progress, human intervention, in one way or another, will still be necessary. Some companies such as Toyota have reintroduced humans into production alongside robots in a continuous quality improvement process.

Another problem seems to be of concern: military applications and more specifically "killer drones". This must be the subject of a real democratic debate. The decision to kill a human should not be made by an algorithm.

Can robots escape the control of humans, or even take power? For me, the answer is no. This is a fantasy that probably relies on imagery from American science fiction films.

6.1.5. *Challenges for researchers*

Robotics is a multidisciplinary science that mobilizes many research teams, public laboratories and companies. Here are some lines of research:

– **mobile robots**: perception and modeling of the environment in order to interact with it; navigation in unknown environments *a priori*; methodologies for perception and decision-making, taking into consideration aspects of autonomy, cooperation and social interaction;

– **interactions**: use of situation models (using a variety of sensors, including computer vision, acoustic perception, tactile sensing and other sensors) for interaction with intelligent objects and companion robots (related to neuroscience); collaborative and heterogeneous robots interacting in living environments;

– **brain modeling and simulation** (in conjunction with neuroscience researchers);

– **learning**: study of the mechanisms that allow robots to learn new skills to be able to interact in initially unknown and changing physical and social environments;

– **cobots**: analysis and modeling of behavior (in connection with human sciences), operator/cobot coupling;

– **understanding the interactions** between robots and humans to facilitate their acceptance (work at the confluence of robotics and psychology).

6.2. Virtual reality and augmented reality

My years at Irisa allowed me to work with researchers and engineers who develop software and deploy applications based on what we call **virtual reality** (VR for short). It seems useful to me to reposition this scientific and technological field, and show that it is complex and has multiple facets.

This term has become fashionable with the widespread distribution of video-headsets. But watching a film or video at 360 degrees with a video-headset is not considered VR by researchers. Indeed, this configuration lacks several components such as, mainly, the possibility to directly interact with the content.

Here is a definition: "Virtual reality is the set of sciences and technologies that allow a user to feel present and interact in an artificial environment. Thus the purpose of virtual reality is to allow one or more users a sensory-motor and cognitive activity in an artificial world, created digitally, which can be imaginary, symbolic or a simulation of certain aspects of the real world."

Two concepts are at the basis of VR: **immersion**, that is, the use of stereoscopy, eye tracking and other techniques to give the illusion that one is inside a synthetic landscape, and **interaction**, that is, the possibility for the user to move around and inside the modeled objects, be it a molecule or an entire city, and to interact with these objects.

6.2.1. *A bit of history*

The very first immersive VR system dates back to the 1950s with Morton Heilig's Sensorama, which already allowed the display of stereoscopic images, sound, smell and motion effects for a multi-sensory user experience.

Ivan Sutherland proposed the concept of Ultimate Display from 1965 to 1970, with a first prototype of a visualization helmet controlled by facial movements. He is the co-founder, with David Evans, of the company Evans & Sutherland specialized in graphics software and simulation.

In 1983, Jaron Lanier and Thomas Zimmerman invented the Dataglove, a fabric glove with optical fibers that let more or less light through depending on the angle when bending the fingers; in 1984, they founded the company VPL, which designed and marketed the first complete VR equipment.

In 1984, Michael McGreevy piloted the Virtual Workstation program at NASA in preparation for the exploration of the planet Mars. This NASA program was continued by Scott Fisher, another major VR inventor, with, in particular, the integration of several interfaces: VPL gloves, HMD (head-mounted display), 3D audio system, etc. Scott Fisher then founded

Telepresence Research, a company specializing in consulting and implementation of virtual environment and telepresence systems for industry and leisure.

At the end of the 1990s, VR began to convince large industrial groups, for example, in the automotive or aeronautics sectors. Since then, VR applications have become affordable for small and medium enterprises.

6.2.2. Hardware configurations of virtual reality

6.2.2.1. Immersive rooms

The CAVE (Cave Automatic Virtual Environment) is undoubtedly the solution offering the most impressive VR immersion.

A user can move around within a cube, the size of a room, whose six faces are backlit screens. On these screens are projected two images presenting two slightly shifted points of view (of the interocular distance) of the same scene. Wearing appropriate glasses enables associating a point of view to each eye to offer an omnidirectional stereoscopic vision to the user. Other devices such as data gloves or haptic arms (force feedback arms) allow the user to interact in the environment. A set of algorithms and software allows a realistic and interactive physical simulation to immerse the user in the 3D virtual environment with which he/she interacts.

Figure 6.2. An SAS Cube (source: Bruno Arnaldi, Irisa). For a color version of this figure, see www.iste.co.uk/delhaye/computing.zip

Developed at the University of Illinois in 1992, the CAVE was the world's first VR technology that allowed multiple users to immerse themselves in the same virtual environment at the same time. On the other hand, not only is this type of system complex to configure, but it also has a high cost.

To meet (in part) the constraints of cost and space, an intermediate system has been developed: the SAS Cube, consisting of a floor projection surface and three vertical projection panels.

6.2.2.2. *The workbench*

The workbench is one of the lightest configurations based on projections on large screens. It is composed of two large rear-projected screens that form an L. Ideal for interactive manipulation, this configuration offers semi-immersive visualization. It fits into the work environment like a drawing table. The projection, stereoscopy and head movement recording technologies are the same as for a CAVE.

They are used for scientific visualization, as well as in the automotive industry.

6.2.2.3. *Head-mounted displays*

Opaque headsets were the first and virtually the only VR configuration in existence until the early 1990s. While military applications have long been instrumental in advancing this technology, it is now being used in a variety of civilian applications. Visualization is carried out on two small screens, each placed in front of one eye.

The semi-transparent headsets of optical technology propose a superimposition of the virtual on reality thanks to an optical system which makes it possible to see reality by semi-transparency. Unlike project-based virtual environments, reality is here necessarily behind the virtual and therefore cannot hide the virtual.

6.2.2.4. *Other common devices*

The dataglove is a sensor-filled glove that allows a user to almost naturally grasp a virtual object and manipulate it, by digitizing the hand's movements in real time.

A force feedback (haptic) arm allows users to design, model and manipulate objects in a virtual environment with tactile (touch) and kinesthetic (force feedback) perception.

The 3D mouse is a six-dimensional pointing device: three translation and three rotation. Compared to the traditional mouse that translates a two-dimensional input movement, the 3D mouse brings depth.

6.2.3. *Fields of use of virtual reality*

The applications of VR are numerous and in full expansion.

6.2.3.1. *Reconstitution*

VR has made it possible to reconstitute many buildings that have disappeared partially or totally, for example, abbeys (Clairvaux, Cluny, etc.). The 3D reconstruction of the Boullongne, a ship of the East India Company launched in 1758, based on plans and historical data, allows historians to discover the real living conditions on board.

With 3D glasses on your face, you can survey the deck and holds as if the ship was real, and even take the helm to steer the boat and climb the mast. This work was done in the SAS Cube of the Immersia VR room (Irisa/ Inria) of the Beaulieu university campus in Rennes.

6.2.3.2. *In the medical field*

A virtual environment can facilitate the education of nurses, taking into account interpersonal relationships and cognitive aspects. Multidisciplinarity is very common in the design of VR applications. VR can be very useful for surgical or dental simulation, as well as for re-education and rehabilitation.

We can also think of applications in psychotherapy. VR techniques have been tested and evaluated in order to treat certain phobias: fear of spiders, vertigo, fear of flying, social phobia, etc. The patient is subjected to dynamic and interactive 3D stimuli, and his/her cognitive, behavioral and functional performance can then be evaluated and treated.

6.2.3.3. *In the industry*

In various fields, such as automotive and aviation, engineers use VR for engine and part design, reducing testing. VR thus complements modeling and simulation software.

Operators can use the same technology to practice before they start using a new machine, saving time on the production line. The entire workstation is modeled in a realistic 3D that immerses the learner and can integrate the simulation of situations such as incidents, anomalies, etc.

6.2.3.4. *Some examples in other areas*

Other examples of VR applications include the following:

– architecture and urban planning: the design of a building in its environment and in all its details, including the evolution of natural lighting at different hours of the day;

– scientific data mining: interactive visualization of complex tridimensional data in geology, visualization and interaction to model new molecules, etc.;

– the military field: simulation of military exercises, training in mine clearance operations, etc.;

– leisure: the video game industry will play a driving role in the development of the VR market, as well as sports (gesture improvement, etc.), tourism (such as visiting the Cheops pyramid in VR) and other types of leisure.

6.2.4. *Augmented reality*

Augmented reality (AR) aims to increase the perception of an individual by adding elements in his/her field of vision that allow him/her a better understanding of his/her environment.

While VR is based on the creation of an environment, AR is based on a real environment because it involves the visualization of a real image (most often the user's immediate physical environment) on which virtual objects are superimposed. AR enables embedding or superimposing the real scene of a video stream captured by a camera virtual still or animated images in real time. The term AR is not entirely accurate because it is not reality that is augmented, but rather the user's perception. It is therefore two different approaches despite the proximity of the two names. A particular difficulty of AR is related to the constraint of having to perfectly position these virtual objects inside the real images (we talk about tracking technologies or position tracking).

AR and VR applications overlap in part. For AR, these include, in particular:

– industry and maintenance (showing thumbnails of the object to be repaired, as well as the operations and location of the maintenance to be carried out);

– tourism (visiting a museum or castle with an AR application is becoming quite common);

– medicine (assistance to the medical gesture);

– advertising (insertion of advertising inserts in video sequences shot in companies, stores or during a soccer match);

– commerce: the furniture sector uses AR to allow customers to visualize furniture in their own interiors through a mobile application;

– games: the spectator is plunged into the heart of a partially real world. Some games, such as the famous location-based *Pokémon Go,* are based on AR.

The advent of smartphones and tablets has made the miniaturization of these devices possible: camera, screen and embedded computing have enabled the development of truly mobile and relevant applications. AR can pose a safety problem: for example, a cyclist wearing AR glasses can be distracted by the information displayed on the screen and risk an accident.

6.3. Health

In 1945, the World Health Organization (WHO) defined health as follows: "A state of complete physical, mental and social well-being and not merely the absence of disease or infirmity." As health is a key societal and economic issue, health actors have sought to use information and communication technologies to improve our well-being and the effectiveness of the care provided by health professionals. As this is a very vast field, we will distinguish here between medical informatics, which is therefore linked to illness, and the contributions of informatics to daily life.

6.3.1. *Health informatics*

E-health (or digital health) refers to "the application of information and communication technologies to all health-related activities".

6.3.1.1. *Technological computing*

Embedded technologies in medical devices have led to significant improvements in diagnosis and care processes.

Medical imaging, discussed in Chapter 5, is probably the oldest computer technology used in medicine; it has progressed considerably over the last 20 years. Discovered more than a century ago, radiography uses X-rays. Ultrasonography is a technique for exploring the inside of the body based on ultrasound. The scanner also uses X-rays; it scans the area to be explored and reconstructs "slices" of the body. Magnetic resonance imaging (MRI) allows you to visualize invisible details on standard X-rays, ultrasound or CT scan. And there are many other techniques! The images can be computer-processed to obtain a 3D representation of an organ, an animation showing its evolution, etc. They allow a better diagnosis and facilitate surgical interventions when necessary.

Robot-assisted surgery, introduced in the 1980s, is now recognized for its great advantage and is spreading in hospitals. A surgical robot is essentially a system to assist the surgeon's gesture; it can be coupled with a medical imaging system. The instruments are directed with extreme precision and the robot can be used to facilitate access to difficult areas, limiting the risk of complications and allowing a faster recovery for patients. Remote telesurgery operations are now possible using sophisticated robots during surgical procedures where doctor and patient are in different locations. Physician expertise and robot technology can be combined using VR and sensors.

Telemedicine connects one or more healthcare professionals to each other or to a patient. It covers several types of acts: **teleconsultation** allows a medical professional to give a remote consultation, **tele-expertise** allows a medical professional to seek the advice of one or more professionals remotely, **telemonitoring** allows a medical professional to remotely interpret data collected from the patient's living place and medical **teleassistance** aims to allow a medical professional to remotely assist another health professional during the performance of an act. Telemedicine is particularly useful for people who are far away from health professionals.

6.3.1.2. *Information technology in the service of coordinated patient care*

The Vitale health card, the first version of which dates back to 1998, is a smart card that certifies citizens' rights to French health insurance. It contains only administrative information. In 2019, the French Ministry of Health announced the launch of a trial of the Health Insurance e-card, an application that can be downloaded from a smartphone or tablet.

The addition of a medical record had been considered, but was abandoned in favor of an ambitious new project, the Shared Medical Record (*dossier medical partagé,* DMP), a digital health record that has been operational since 2011. Confidential and secure, it stores online health information (care history, medical history such as allergies, test results, hospitalization reports, etc.). It enables this information to be shared with attending physicians and all the healthcare professionals who take care of patients, even in hospital. It can be consulted on a website or via a smartphone application.

6.3.1.3. *Information technology at the service of documentation and knowledge*

Healthcare professionals have access, via the Internet, to many sources of information. But we can all find documentation on health problems that concern us by using search engines.

In all countries, health data is growing exponentially; it is the Big Data phenomenon we have already spoken about. These data have very different typologies (clinical, biological, social, behavioral, demographic, etc.) and also very different formats (text, numerical value, signal, 2D and 3D images, genomic sequence, etc.). Finally, they come from a variety of sources: medical records, clinical trials, administrative databases, patient data (connected objects, applications), social networks, etc. The implementation of coherent databases is an important issue for all healthcare stakeholders. Data Mining or artificial intelligence methods can be used to analyze these large amounts of data, for example, for research organizations, healthcare manufacturers, epidemiological surveillance or diagnostic support.

In France, the *Système national des données de santé* (SNDS), effective since April 2017, brings together the main existing public health databases. The SNDS aims to improve knowledge on medical care and to broaden the scope of research, studies and evaluations in the field of health. It connects health insurance and hospital data, medical causes of death and data relating to disability.

The creation of the Health Data Hub, planned for 2021, is part of a dynamic of enrichment of the SNDS. Its objective is to promote usage and multiply the possibilities for exploiting health data. It will enable the development of new techniques, in particular those related to artificial intelligence methods. It will also have a role in promoting innovation in the use of health data. The structuring of digital health data and their semantic coding is one of the key elements in the Health Data Hub's supply.

6.3.2. *Information technology at the service of our health*

Our health can benefit daily from information technology.

Connected objects can help people to get to know each other better, to monitor and improve their health. The most common objects are watches and bracelets to measure the number of steps and kilometers traveled, the speed and type of travel, the level of sun exposure, heart rate, blood pressure, etc. Others, more sophisticated, are aids for people who are ill or who have just undergone surgery: a pillbox that sends an alert signal (sound, SMS) if you forget to take your treatment, connected patches for Alzheimer's patients allowing them to be geo-located, devices that detect a fall of a dependent person and send an alert. More recently, there are trials of drugs containing a sensor in the pill that emits a signal when ingested, and makes it possible to know when the patient has taken his or her treatment. There is no shortage of conceivable applications.

Robots make life easier for elderly and/or dependent people who wish to stay at home as long as possible, as we have already seen. They can also simplify hospitalization at home, and intervene in the treatment of illnesses such as autism, as various experiments have shown.

Another example of the contribution of IT in the health field is the use of AR glasses allowing visually impaired people to regain some independence.

The connection of all these devices is of course essential because it allows the collection of data, some of which can be used by medical staff.

6.4. The connected (and soon autonomous?) car

Computers appeared in vehicles in the late 1980s. Today, the automotive industry is one of the sectors that make extensive use of on-board technologies, combining pure computing (programming, design of applications) and electronics (sensors, interfaces, etc.). On average, there are between 40 and 60 computers in cars, and up to 80 for high-end models, integrating data transmission systems. A mid-range car can carry about 150–200 million lines of code.

Engines, temperature sensors, vehicle air conditioning, on-board controls, navigation devices, radar (reversing or more), braking assistance (ABS), voice recognition, permanent vehicle diagnostics, leisure equipment and park assist are increasingly common. The passenger compartment should also become more intelligent and more comfortable (air purity, temperature, lighting, ambient fragrances) depending on the conditions detected: pollution, heat and mood of the occupants.

The first tests of an autonomous (and therefore driverless) car date back to the late 1970s. In the 1980s, research labs specializing in robotics tested prototypes, but it was not until 2010 that the subject became media headlines when Google announced that it was working on this technology, first with modified production vehicles and then with the Google Car designed entirely by Google. Other companies have embarked on projects, such as Uber or the manufacturer Tesla. A few accidents, including two fatalities, made the headlines, but we forget the thousands of deaths on the roads each year in France alone! Now the time has come to focus on autonomous shuttles operating in a secure environment, away from traffic, even if experiments are still being carried out on open roads.

This is a huge market and all the big names in the IT and automotive industries are working in this sector, not to mention a myriad of start-ups. The connected car is not yet a standalone car; there is still a lot to be done and the manufacturers are getting ready, forging alliances among themselves and with the GAFA.

Various studies have been published on this subject, for example, by the CEA[2], Inria[3] or the University of Cambridge[4].

6.4.1. *Levels of autonomy*

There are generally six levels of autonomy:

– level 0: no autonomy, the driver is in full control of his/her vehicle. Only warning mechanisms such as a back-up radar or an alert linked to an anomaly support the user;

– level 1: the driver remains permanently responsible for the maneuvers but delegates certain tasks to the system. Power steering technologies, such as lane departure radar, may also be introduced, as well as collision warning;

– level 2: limited autonomy; the trajectory of the car (longitudinal and lateral movements) is ensured by the system. The car can be equipped with driving aids such as park assist, which allows the car to automatically park with or without the help of the driver;

– level 3: vehicles begin to understand the environment around them by detecting specific road features such as other people's cars, the road and lines on the ground. The steering system is responsible for keeping the vehicle in its lane while maintaining a speed that is appropriate for the authorized speed and traffic conditions. The driver supervises the vehicle and can regain control of the vehicle if necessary. Some cars are at this level of autonomy;

– level 4: highly automated level in which the driver is no longer involved. The trajectory is automatically managed and the car monitors its environment to guarantee safety even in the event of a failure or unforeseen event. However, driving automation is limited to certain roads such as freeways and to conventional weather conditions. Level 4 cars are not yet on the roads and are still in the prototype stage;

---

2 http://www.cea.fr/comprendre/Pages/nouvelles-technologies/essentiel-sur-voiture-autonome. aspx.

3 https://www.inria.fr/sites/default/files/2019-10/inrialivreblancvac-180529073843.pdf.

4 https://www.newn.cam.ac.uk/wp-content/uploads/2019/07/Allen-Emma-2.iii_pdf.

– level 5: complete autonomy; the vehicle can travel without the intervention of a physical person, on any type of road. Everything is under the responsibility and control of the computer system. The very presence of a human being at the controls is no longer necessary.

6.4.2. *Challenges associated with the autonomous car*

We have mentioned several times the growing importance of electronics, software and communication systems in vehicles, especially in cars. For a vehicle to be able to circulate in a totally autonomous way, without any human intervention, it must be able to 1) perceive its environment, 2) analyze and interpret the data it receives, 3) make the right decisions on how to drive the vehicle, all this with 4) guaranteed operational safety.

6.4.2.1. *The perception of the environment*

The autonomous vehicle must be able to identify all fixed or mobile objects in its environment (signs, pedestrians, other vehicles, etc.), to predict the evolution of mobile objects, to establish a map of its environment and to locate itself in it. To do this, the car must be equipped with a multitude of sensors: cameras operating in the visible and infrared, radars, lasers such as lidars (light detection and ranging) and ultrasonic sensors. It is of course essential to process in real time the data coming from these sensors and to merge them, because the information given by sensors of different physical nature complements each other, thus obtaining relevant information.

6.4.2.2. *Interpretation of the data*

Computer software will give meaning to the data collected. This software has first undergone a learning phase, using deep learning technologies, to be able to correctly analyze the external environment and recognize, for example, a face or understand a road sign. It has also learned to memorize numerous scenarios. Methods have been developed to refine the location of the vehicle with an accuracy of the order of a meter or even a decimeter.

6.4.2.3. *Decision-making*

Depending on the result of the analysis of the data by the software, the fully autonomous car has to make a driving decision. Here too, the software plays a central role in choosing the route to be taken or the maneuver to be carried out (braking, etc.).

6.4.2.4. *Reliability of operation*

The operational reliability of all the bodies mentioned is of course essential in this context. It relies first of all on redundancy of sensors (a sensor can have a problem). As software is at the heart of decisions, it must be validated by formal methods of proof (we refer to Chapter 3 devoted to software). Finally, communications between the car, other vehicles and the environment must be efficient and reliable, taking into account the diversity of networks (cellular, Wi-Fi, Bluetooth, etc.).

6.4.3. *Advantages and disadvantages of the autonomous car*

The arrival of the autonomous vehicle will have advantages and disadvantages, and will have an impact on society, for example, on the organization of urban space.

Everyone agrees on a reduction in the number of accidents, as the vehicle is not likely to be under the influence of alcohol, to fall asleep, to speed, etc. The road network should be safer and traffic should flow more smoothly, but the road infrastructure will need to be adapted. There will be less time lost for those who spend a lot of time in their cars, especially in traffic jams. Carpooling will be facilitated, as autonomous vehicles can easily pick up their users, thus reducing overall energy consumption.

The arrival of the autonomous car brings not only advantages but also challenges. How will the large amounts of data produced by these systems be secured and used? Who will own the data collected? Who will be able to know that I went on such and such a day at such and such a time to such and such an address? It will have an effect on the labor market: truck, bus and cab drivers will be directly concerned because their jobs could disappear in the long term. The question of cyber security will arise: hackers can already find the frequency emitted by car keys at a distance (within a radius of about 10 meters) and can penetrate or even steal them; with autonomous cars, computer hacking, targeted against one vehicle or an entire fleet simultaneously, will be a major risk. The transfer of responsibility for the driver's driving to the manufacturer or manufacturers of components of the autonomous vehicle will be a question for lawyers and insurers.

And, finally, how will the population receive it? The extra cost will be high (several tens of thousands of euros, at least initially). Are we ready to entrust ourselves to a vehicle over which we have no control? More simply, the pleasure of driving, which exists for many people, will disappear.

6.5. The smart city

Massive urbanization poses many problems, both for those in charge and for the inhabitants. The aim is to improve the quality of life of city dwellers, reduce costs and energy consumption by making the city more adaptive and efficient, using new information and communication technologies. This concept is not new. The pioneering cities in this field are the megacities of Asia, such as Hong Kong or Singapore. Since then, hundreds of cities around the world, including France, have launched programs with this objective.

New information and communication technologies (home automation, smart sensors and meters, digital media, information devices, networks, etc.) will be at the heart of the city of tomorrow. This concept of the smart city is very global, and each city can focus its intelligence on aspects such as energy savings, public transportation, innovative projects, communication between citizens and their elected officials, etc. There is no single model for a smart city, because all cities draw on their history, geography and multiple specificities.

Figure 6.3. *Various aspects of the smart city (source: Jean-Loïc Delhaye).*
For a color version of this figure, see www.iste.co.uk/delhaye/computing.zip

We are going to give some concrete examples showing the role of information technology in these innovations that can make cities smarter and more at the service of their citizens. The reader who is interested in this subject in a global way will be able to consult with interest Francis Pisani's report *"Voyage dans les villes intelligentes : entre datapolis et participolis[5]"*.

6.5.1. *Smart energy*

Saving energy and reducing the carbon footprint are among the objectives of all cities. Better energy management is possible: diversifying energy sources and managing them in a global and optimized way thanks to a smart grid; taking advantage of local resources (every territory has local natural energy resources); wind, sun, waves, ground heat, biomass are free sources of energy that are just waiting to be exploited.

Some cities are getting smart street lamps. Equipped with LEDs instead of conventional bulbs, they consume less. Sensors are also installed to detect the proximity of pedestrians. When the streets are empty, the brightness is dimmed to consume less energy. They also collect information on the level of air pollution, noise level and provide Wi-Fi access to passers-by. The information provided is centralized and allows for better overall management.

The Internet of Things and data analysis can be used to optimize energy consumption inside public buildings, for example, by adapting lighting and heating to the lifestyle of their occupants.

6.5.2. *Smart buildings*

The applications of computing are numerous, from the individual home to office buildings or factories, and we have mentioned several with the Internet of Things or robots.

We can say that home automation brings together technologies in the field of electronics, information and telecommunications, designed to make a

---

5 http://data.over-blog-kiwi.com/0/73/87/12/20150402/ob_955cef_ob-094dfc-pisani-voyage danslesvillesin.pdf.

house smarter. It provides functions related to comfort, energy management, home security, etc.

Let us imagine a smart house in a certain future. I have been woken up by soft music, the atmosphere in the room set as well as possible. The shutters have opened automatically. I go to take my shower whose flow and temperature are adapted to my wishes (these parameters will be different for my wife). Meanwhile, breakfast has been prepared and I can see the news I have programmed (weather, national and international news). Once dressed, I find my car (autonomous perhaps) which has also been prepared (temperature, atmosphere), the garage has opened and will close again as soon as I am gone. Once the last inhabitant has left, the heating will be adjusted to optimize energy consumption and the alarm system will be activated. The cleaning will then be done by robots and the washing machine will choose the right program by analyzing the laundry it contains. I can make sure that my children have arrived at school and I will be able to verify that they came home on time. If something happens in the house, I will be informed in real time on my smartphone. A drone delivers my lunch to me at the exact time I choose. When I get home, the garage opens, and the security system was deactivated when the first member of the family arrived. The groceries were delivered and the house was set to "evening mode", with a warm atmosphere (lights, temperature, music). After dinner, we have sophisticated multimedia systems that allow everyone to do what they want to do: watch a movie, play with the family or network, chat with a friend, etc. When I decide to go to bed, my environment adapts, unused rooms are turned off and the appropriate alarms are activated.

Of course, some of these functions are also useful in any type of building. You can also imagine what life can be like in the office, what life can be like for the children at school, how other activities such as sports will be carried out, etc. Science fiction? Not totally, because some of these functions already exist. And, do we want to experience this type of scenario?

6.5.3. *Smart infrastructure*

The first question that arises concerns architecture and urban design. What kind of urbanization do we want? Do we give carte blanche to real estate developers and companies? This question arises as soon as a city plans the renovation of a neighborhood. It is a question of inventing new ways of working together and designing the city. Home, employment, shops and leisure activities must be approached in a coherent way, limiting passenger transportation and thus reducing the energy and environmental impact of mobility. We will discuss mobility again in section 6.6.

The equipment must be accessible by everyone, with smartphones making it possible to locate it and find the best way to access it according to each person's constraints.

Networks (water, sewers, etc.) can be better managed thanks to sensors that detect leaks and alert maintenance departments. The waste collection services know in real time the level of filling of the containers, thanks to sensors, which allows them to optimize the rounds.

6.5.4. *Smart governance*

A virtual public service assistant can help and respond to constituents who may encounter problems in the course of their day-to-day activities, such as renewing their identity card or registering for school.

Urban signage is an effective means of communicating with citizens, with technologies that allow information to be tailored to certain characteristics such as the age, gender and areas of interest of the people viewing the sign. Customization of the information is possible.

Communication between citizens and city officials can be made easier, in particular thanks to smartphones: reporting an incident, receiving an alert on the air quality in a particular neighborhood depending on the person's frailty, etc.

The fight against noise pollution is facilitated by the installation of sensors, for example, on street lamps, whose signals are continuously analyzed. Personal safety is also part of governance for local authorities. Camera networks are only one facet, and the analysis of the numerous data collected (history of events, messages from inhabitants, local contexts) should enable the anticipation of possible difficulties.

6.5.5. *Dangers*

Does the smart city outline a multi-speed city? The increasing digitization of cities risks creating new inequalities. It increases the risk of exclusion for certain groups of people, caused by the dematerialization of urban services and administrative procedures.

Smart cities raise other issues, such as data governance and privacy. The smart city is driven by data. Optimizing urban management, inventing new services and responding to the individual needs of residents relies on the collection, storage and processing of increasingly massive amounts of data. To a large extent, even if the data is subsequently anonymized or aggregated, it is personal data. The implementation of an ethical charter to establish rules for data exchange and sharing is necessary. It is a matter of putting in place the necessary safeguards to ensure that this evolution towards smarter cities is in the interest of all and not just for the benefit of a few.

This also raises the question of cyber security. Because of the growing number of devices (connected objects, etc.) and data traffic, smart cities are exposed to many potential security breaches that can impact not only their urban infrastructures, but also hospitals, transportation systems or all kinds of structures they manage.

6.6. Smart mobility

Whether in the city or in the countryside, mobility is too often associated with congestion, the difficulty of finding efficient means of transport, pollution, the cost of individual transport (vehicle, fuel, tolls) or public transport, wasted time, and so on. People who are isolated, elderly or disabled are finding it increasingly difficult to get around. Some large cities are introducing measures such as alternate traffic patterns or city tolls. Local authorities are seeking to improve the mobility of citizens; IT and telecommunications can help implement solutions leading to what is called smart mobility.

Limiting the construction of new infrastructure by optimizing the use and performance of existing transportation systems, improving road safety, enhancing service quality through real-time information, reducing inequalities that offer opportunities for mobility for all, and ensuring environmental protection: these are the main areas of application of ITS

(**Intelligent Transportation Systems**). Many cities have launched projects that use new information and communication technologies.

The **Mobility 3.0** initiative, led by the ATEC ITS France association, which promotes exchanges and experiences between mobility professionals, is the expression of the desire of French players to take up the digital challenge and fulfill its promises in terms of traffic optimization, economic performance, respect for the environment, quality of life, the fight against climate change and road safety.

Ad hoc solutions exist. The operating plans of traffic lights automatically adapted according to the traffic allow them to regulate it (sensors, communication with the vehicles). Improving the operation of public transportation, including autonomous shuttles at sites where they are a plus, reduces the use of private cars. User information can be improved: knowing in real time where I can find an available place to park, thus freeing up traffic and saving fuel, or where to find the nearest free terminal to recharge my electric vehicle. In Santander in northern Spain, the city has created an AR application that allows anyone to point their smartphone at a street in the city to view the bus stops available nearby, the lines that stop there and the delay before the next bus passes.

If the solutions proposed in the city are not easily transposable to the countryside, innovative ideas adapted to the particular context must be found.

The concept of **MaaS** (Mobility as a Service), born in 2014 in Scandinavia, is based on the principle of conceiving mobility as a service that allows people to go from point A to point B. Like a personal assistant, a smartphone application offers the fastest, cheapest or most comfortable routes, these routes being combinations of multiple modes of transportation, whether public, private or shared (autonomous cabs, metro, carpooling, self-service bicycles, etc.), all with a single subscription and platform, as is the case in Île-de-France with the Navigo card. This requires strong coordination between transportation operators (public or private, cabs, VTC, self-service bicycles, etc.) and companies that integrate their different services. One of the success factors of intermodality is information, and a predictive layer is needed in the applications to anticipate the availability of each mode and guide the user to the most relevant mode of transport at the time of request. Data and predictive algorithms will play a decisive role in making mobility ever more active, fluid and connected. Operators, integrators and a number of start-ups are working to make this concept a reality.

6.7. The factory of the future

Industry 4.0, the factory of the future, the intelligent factory... So many terms to describe this new model of factory born from the 4th Industrial Revolution, following three major phases of evolution called revolutions: mechanization, driven by the steam engine (half of the 18th century), mass production, driven by electrical energy (half of the 19th century) and automation, supported by electronics and computers (half of the 20th century).

The 4th Industrial Revolution organizes production processes induced by innovations linked to the Internet of Things and digital technologies. Industry 4.0 corresponds in a way to the digitization of the factory. The objectives are numerous: to respond to the growing demand for personalized products from consumers, to respond to current issues of resource and energy management, to optimize and make production cycles more flexible, to create a logistics process capable of rapidly exchanging company information with all its partners, etc. But it fails to recognize that reducing employment is also part of these objectives.

6.7.1. *Technologies*

The factory of the future is based on many interconnected technologies related to digital technology, which we have already discussed in previous chapters.

Robots will play an increasingly important role; they will be more autonomous and will communicate with each other and with humans. Cobots, or collaborative robots, will assist human operators. All are equipped with sensors and software.

The design of a new product will increasingly involve **numerical modeling** (structure, materials), simulation of its behavior and qualities (resistance, etc.). Computer-aided design and manufacturing tools (CAD/CAM) are now widespread. This considerably reduces the time and cost of product development, often avoiding the often lengthy prototyping phase. This modeling can be applied to the entire production process.

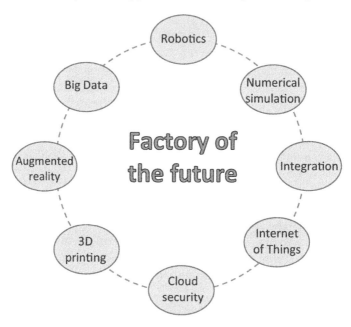

Figure 6.4. *Technologies for the factory of the future*

The factory of the future encourages a new form of collaboration, articulating **vertical integration** (integration of players throughout the value chain, from supplier to customer) and **horizontal integration** (reinforced collaboration between different departments, from marketing to quality control). Information sharing is therefore essential.

The **connected objects**, embedded on parts, machines and globally in all stages of the production cycle, provide a large amount of information facilitating the monitoring of production rates, reaction to incidents and machine maintenance.

The **Cloud** enables users to benefit from the computing and storage power of remote computer servers, at lower costs than those of internal IT systems. It must ensure the **security and integrity of all the data** that can be transferred between the different systems.

Additive manufacturing, also known as **3D printing,** allows the production of complex, custom-shaped parts in record time and with great precision.

AR can facilitate industrial maintenance. VR allows the development of manufacturing processes and facilitates the training of the personnel who will contribute to them.

All of these technologies require data and produce **large amounts of data** that must be able to be analyzed in real time. The role of data and communication systems is therefore essential in the factory of the future.

6.7.2. *Issues*

The objectives of Industry 4.0 are associated with several major issues:

– **the competitiveness of companies**: those that do not take this path risk having factories from the past and being put out of business. Many companies, large and small, have taken steps in this direction, particularly in fields such as aeronautics and the automotive industry. Renault, for example, created Renault Digital in 2017, an entity responsible for delivering digital projects for all of the company's businesses;

– **the adaptation of the company's organization**: the company must transform itself by involving the stakeholders that are the employees, suppliers and customers. It is a question of rethinking management and more particularly that of human resources. As professions evolve, staff training is essential to support them in this transition, and new professions are emerging;

– **vigilance on safety**: the factory of the future requires production systems with high requirements in terms of reliability, availability and robustness. In addition, access to production-related data and services must be controllable to protect the company's know-how. Finally, strict measures must protect access to systems, as hackers may seek to block production;

– **an important environmental role**: with resources becoming scarcer, climate change and the energy transition gradually being initiated in all countries, Factory 4.0 needs more than ever to have a very small ecological footprint. The digitization of the industry seems to open up many doors to achieve this goal.

6.7.3. *The place of the human*

Is this vision of the factory of the future optimistic? The issues presented above are not simple and correspond to challenges that will have to be met. But where do human beings fit into this vision?

Beyond its technical advances, Industry 4.0 will be marked by a complete disruption of the productive process, the disappearance of medium-skilled jobs and their replacement by automatons. The appearance of new professions (computer scientists, engineers, network experts, etc.) will not compensate for the disappearance and will have to be accompanied by intensive and long-term training. Work and paces will be controlled by algorithms. There will be new modes of collaboration and cooperation between employees. The quality of social dialogue will be essential in this change.

Today's factory is also a social space in which the staff rub shoulders, exchange ideas in front of the coffee machine and build solidarity. What will the factory of the future be like?

7

Societal Issues

This last chapter is not devoted to technology but offers a look at some of the questions that the massive presence of information and communication technologies in all sectors of our lives seemingly poses to society.

What are the threats of cybercrime? Does the uncontrolled use of our multiple forms of personal information threaten our privacy? Is social life under influence? Is democracy in danger? Are we all participants in this digital world? Are AI applications risk-free? Will intelligent prostheses create a category of bionic humans? Can we envisage an increase in our life expectancy, or even our immortality? Finally, what kind of society do we want?

7.1. Security

We have mentioned computer security (often referred to as cybersecurity) in several of the chapters of this book, particularly in Chapter 2 on networks. We would like to insist here on the questions it raises when several billion computers are connected worldwide, and soon, probably tens of billions of connected objects: theft of strategic information, spying, ransomware attacks, sabotage of essential operators (banks, health, energy) and destabilization relayed by social networks.

7.1.1. *Specific characteristics*

Computer security is a set of technologies, processes and practices designed to protect networks, computers and data against attacks, damage and unauthorized access that can be grouped under the term cybercrime.

Attacks can be mounted remotely. Local law is usually powerless in the face of assaults from afar; international cooperation is often complex and slow. Attacks are easily automated and large-scale. They can hit targets very quickly anywhere in the world, affecting virtually every sector of our activities (health, commerce, finance, defense, etc.).

Attackers remain anonymous quite easily. Sometimes, even the geographical origin of attacks is difficult to establish: does an attack really come from China, or is it a Russian attack that transits through bots (automatic or semi-automatic software agents that interact with computer servers) in China? Or maybe it is a mixture of both? The possible sanctions therefore have less deterrent power.

7.1.2. *Some great threats*

7.1.2.1. *Attacks on economic targets*

A significant proportion of computer attacks for spying purposes target players in the economic, scientific or industrial sector. The aim is to penetrate computer systems in order to steal patents or create data leaks. The attacker's objective is to discreetly maintain access for as long as possible in order to capture strategic information in a timely manner. Recent examples have shown that organizations such as NASA in the United States are not immune to these cyber attacks.

Saturation attacks are another way to destabilize a company. It usually involves flooding a server with unnecessary requests to overwhelm it and make it inaccessible; this is known as a denial of service, which can be very serious for the organization that is the victim.

7.1.2.2. *Infrastructure attacks*

These are (fortunately quite rare) attacks, which target, for example, a country's communication or electricity network in order to produce a blackout. The simplest way is to carry out a denial of service attack. But the attack can target a few computers with a major role in the infrastructure and introduce a virus that will render them inoperable.

7.1.2.3. *Ransomware campaigns*

Ransomware is malicious software that blocks computers and demands ransom, for example, Bitcoins, in exchange for a return to function. This type of campaign is aimed at both companies and individuals.

This category of attacks includes phishing, which is aimed at obtaining, from the recipient of an apparently legitimate e-mail, the transmission of bank details or login details for financial services, in order to steal money from them. Generally, the e-mail usurps the identity of a legal entity (company, public service, etc.) or a physical person (colleague, friend).

7.1.2.4. *Introduction of viruses into computers*

A computer virus is a self-replicating software program designed to cause more or less drastic damage to the proper functioning of a host computer or computer network. One method of introducing a virus is to invite the recipient to open a malicious attachment or follow a link to a malicious website.

7.1.2.5. *Propaganda and misinformation*

Fake news, or infox, which is not just false news but deliberately falsified and misleading information, is invading the Internet. Disinformation campaigns, which can be initiated by states or leaders, are common.

7.1.2.6. *Cyberwarfare*

The destabilization of democratic and economic processes is among the objectives of cyber attacks. The threats we have just mentioned are elements of cyberwarfare.

To restrict ourselves to the military domain, it is obvious that all weapons (planes, ships, ground vehicles, etc.) are equipped with often complex software and are involved in communication networks. It cannot be ruled out that a weapon system is rendered ineffective by the introduction of malware or viruses into software by an enemy country. The military and secret services of many countries are very active both in organizing cyber defense and cyber attacks. In the summer of 2019, the *New York Times* reported a

US cyber attack against some Iranian computer systems to prevent Iran from attacking oil tankers in the Persian Gulf again.

7.1.3. *Acting to protect oneself*

The societal stakes of cybersecurity are so high that all developed countries have set up agencies in charge of this field. In France, the role of the *Agence nationale de la sécurité des systèmes d'information* (ANSSI) is to facilitate a coordinated consideration of cybersecurity issues. These agencies collaborate at an international level, as it is clear that cyber attacks do not respect borders. They focus their activities on the main threats facing governments, businesses and major public and private organizations.

The majority of companies and public bodies have a manager or even a specialist department responsible for IT security, and they lay down very precise rules adapted to their specific context. But the general public who use IT tools, including smartphones and connected objects, must also be vigilant against attacks from hackers. Let's remind ourselves of some measures we should all take: be vigilant when surfing the Web, use long passwords and change them periodically, never click on a link or open a file from strangers, report suspicious e-mails to an *ad hoc* organization such as Signal Spam.

7.2. The respect of private life

We exchange information with many people, known or unknown, we surf on many websites, exchange messages, use social networks and smartphones, etc. We have become large consumers as well as large producers of information, some of which concerns our private life, but which is likely to be aggregated and accessed by others (individuals, companies, etc.). The idea that only people who have something to hide need to worry about their privacy is a bad idea. How much of our lives should remain private?

7.2.1. *Our personal data*

The data we produce can be retrieved by many means and used without our knowledge by actors who don't always mean well. Here are a few examples.

7.2.1.1. Data theft and leakage

The data that we keep on our computer equipment (computer, smartphone or other) can be stolen by intrusion of a malicious third party. This is also true for what we send to the Cloud, those huge data centers whose security is often compromised. Beware of sensitive data!

Data, sometimes confidential, are stored on various sites. The notorious *Panama Papers* scandal is linked to the leak of more than 11.5 million confidential documents from the Panamanian law firm Mossack Fonseca, detailing information on more than 214,000 companies as well as the names of the shareholders of these companies. In 2018, Facebook announced that the data from 29 million users may have been stolen by attackers of unknown origin. Many recent examples have confirmed that our data are still vulnerable and we only know the tip of the iceberg.

7.2.1.2. Electronic mail

Does e-mail ensure confidentiality? The nature of the Internet means that a message passes through several computers before it reaches its destination. At each station, the message leaves a trace and can be intercepted and read or even modified. Even if interception is prohibited by law, there is no guarantee that a curious person won't take a look at your mail.

7.2.1.3. Navigation on the Web

The operating systems of our computers spy on all human–machine interactions including keystrokes, data from the microphone and even data from the webcam. A cookie is a text file, therefore not a virus, generated by the server of the site you are visiting, which is deposited by your browser on your computer when you surf the Internet. These cookies are used by merchant sites, which is not too serious, but they often record the pages you look at and will store information about your behavior on the Internet. Who will use this information and for what purpose?

7.2.1.4. Smartphones

The smartphone is one of the main vectors for collecting personal information. It communicates information both on our centers of interest, via the applications that we have installed on our smartphones, and on our travels thanks to geolocation.

In August 2019, Google security researchers revealed the existence of 14 vulnerabilities affecting iPhone users, even with up-to-date security patches. Some applications that can be easily downloaded contain malware.

7.2.1.5. *Connected objects*

They are everywhere or almost everywhere (smart TVs, smart refrigerators, robot vacuum cleaners, connected stuffed animals and other voice assistants) and they are slowly invading our homes. But can we trust them? They are objects that are generally very vulnerable from a security point of view. It has been proven that it is possible to take control of the camera and microphone of a smart TV and spy on its owner without their knowledge. A specialist in the field showed how she had managed to exploit a security vulnerability in the famous Karotz multifunctional rabbit she had given to her daughter; this allowed her to take remote control of the device without her knowledge, using a computer, and to use her camera and microphone to spy on her.

7.2.1.6. *Video surveillance, audio surveillance*

Under security pretexts, webcams with biometric recognition invade city streets, train stations and airport halls, tourist spaces; they can even be found on billboards, in the eyes of mannequins in store windows and inside stores, so that anonymity becomes impossible in public space. What about our private life?

In October 2019, the newspaper *Le Monde* reported that the *Commission nationale de l'informatique et des libertés* had sent a letter to the city of Saint-Etienne concerning its project to equip certain streets with microphones to alert the authorities in case of an anomaly. It noted in particular that the continuous and undifferentiated capture of sounds in the public space created the risk of capturing private conversations.

7.2.2. *Uses of our data*

Our data may be of interest to many organizations; here are a few examples.

Commerce makes extensive use of our personal data, through the tracking of our web browsing, our trips to the stores thanks to our smartphones, or thanks to loyalty cards that provide a detail of our purchases.

Many companies share personal information (name, postal address, e-mail, photo, bank details, social network postings, IP address, etc.) of their employees or customers with third parties (suppliers or partners). Some companies use new technologies in an intrusive way: permanent video surveillance of workplaces and living areas or locating employees using the SIM card in their cell phones. Spying, whether by governments or companies (industrial espionage), mainly concerns people in very important positions. Some private confidential data can weaken the position of these people.

Banks and insurance companies are very interested in our private lives, especially data related to our health. Obtaining a bank loan, the premiums of our insurances and our mutual insurance company can be very dependent on these data.

Our personal information may be used for manipulation purposes. We recall the Cambridge Analytica affair, the name of the English company that, following the recovery of millions of pieces of data, drew up and classified psychological profiles of people and then sent them targeted and adapted messages during election campaigns – in particular, Donald Trump's first. Some nations, such as Russia, are also often suspected of manipulation (fake news, etc.).

7.2.3. *What about the future?*

The future of our privacy depends in part on each of us, as well as on legislative measures to limit fraudulent uses. What steps can we take to protect our privacy and what are our rights?

The first step to take is vigilance. It is a matter of avoiding communicating sensitive personal information, in e-mails, on social networks, in Internet browsing, on our smartphones. Let's not forget that we can be identified directly (by our first and last name) as well as from the crossing of a set of data (e.g. a person living at such and such an address, born on such and such a day and a member of such and such an association).

Legislation in this area is evolving. The French Data Protection Act of 1978 reinforces the control by citizens of the use that can be made of data concerning them. The European Union's General Data Protection Regulation

(GDPR)[1], which is the reference text on personal data protection, came into force in 2018. All public bodies, companies and associations that collect personal data on European residents are concerned, including GAFA, Uber, Airbnb, etc. Any processing in breach of the GDPR can lead to sanctions and fines of up to 20 million euros or 4% of the annual turnover of the previous year. Article 17 of the GDPR grants EU citizens a right to the deletion of their personal data, better known to the general public as the "right to be forgotten". This right to dereferencing applies only within the borders of the European Union.

In any case, it will be increasingly difficult to protect our privacy if we are not careful.

7.3. Influence on social life

Remember: not so long ago, about 10 years ago, the Internet was synonymous with freedom of expression, democratization of knowledge and horizontal relationships. One of the major contributions of the Internet is in the field of freedom of communication. This freedom is twofold: it is the right to be informed but above all the right to express oneself. It therefore constitutes a place for debate and allows, through e-mail and the multiplication of forums, websites and then social networks, to confront points of view and exchange information.

What about today?

7.3.1. *The development of social ties*

In the digital age, social networks allow us to communicate across multiple platforms and applications, in a multitude of fields, depending on our interests. The Internet makes it easy to find people who share the same interests. We do not count the apps, professional or cultural, for example, which are being created in recent years. Many associations of all types are created and developed through websites, membership lists, blogs, networks that allow them to make themselves known.

---

1 https://eur-lex.europa.eu/legal-content/EN/TXT/HTML/?uri=CELEX:32016R0679.

More simply, we can easily communicate with our family and friends, wherever they are in the world, thanks to the applications available on our computer or our smartphone: e-mail, video, chat, etc., and all this for free most of the time. This ease does not, however, enhance the quality of human relationships: an e-mail does not replace a face-to-face meeting, because the signs of non-written, non-verbal communication disappear. And I'm always surprised to see people sitting at the same table in a restaurant spending their mealtime consulting their smartphones!

7.3.2. Citizen participation

The Internet promotes greater interaction between those who govern and those who are governed. Many local authorities inform the inhabitants thanks to an application or a dedicated website. The latter can express their ideas on equipment or developments to be carried out on the territory. They can dialogue directly with an elected official or a department, or report a deterioration in their street. It is thus a direct consultation allowed by Internet technologies. We can imagine that the Internet could be a tool to participate in the legislative process by forums open to the Parliament and the sending to the parliamentarians of proposals of amendments. We are witnessing the creation of so-called civic tech initiatives.

In some ways, the Internet promotes collective action, allowing isolated but like-minded individuals to get in touch and mobilize. The *Gilet jaunes* (Yellow Vests) were first organized via Facebook. The Internet allows an alternative flow of information to limit the effects of the power of money in regard to the monopolization of the means of information. On the other hand, the Internet leaves room for disinformation and conspiracy based on the idea that everything is hidden from the citizen by a minority for the purpose of domination. According to some surveys, half of the French say they no longer trust the traditional media and follow the news on the Internet, which is full of false information. Surprising!

7.3.3. The socialization of knowledge

The classic vertical hierarchy of knowledge is giving way to a horizontal organization, under the influence of the Web. I am impressed by the ability of young people to find answers to their questions or to find a book for their e-reader. This is also the case for the immigrants to whom I teach the French language: with their smartphones, they find dictionaries, language learning sites, etc. I often use the Web to find the definition of a term, a director's filmography, etc.

Many sites list, at least partially, the knowledge available in a specific field. Wikipedia is an example of a database, which is furthermore informed by Internet users. But, because there is another side to the coin, this information is generally not filtered and validated, and must be used with some caution and intelligence, for example, in the health field.

7.4. Dangers to democracy

The development of digital technology has many advantages, but it also has negative aspects that should not be underestimated.

7.4.1. *The liberation of speech*

Liberation of speech has not only positive aspects. The Internet can also be the medium for disseminating false or defamatory information about an individual, or actions or ideas that contradict the foundations of democracy. Sites propagating negationist or racist ideas are accessible. There are laws that make it possible to fight against harassment, racist remarks, death threats, etc., but the delegation of regulatory power to private firms pursuing their own economic interests raises the question of the future of freedom of expression. This is all the more so since the States leave these companies a relative autonomy in the exercise of their regulatory power.

7.4.2. *Private life under surveillance*

The digital industry thrives on a simple principle: extract personal data and sell advertisers predictions about user behavior. But for profits to grow, the prognosis must change to certainty. To do this, it is no longer enough to simply predict, it is now a matter of changing human behavior on a large scale.

The Internet becomes a tool at the service of mass surveillance, and the big companies, which said they were pursuing a liberal and libertarian project of citizen emancipation, appear to be pursuing economic interests that contribute to this surveillance. Edward Snowden's revelations in 2013 about the NSA (National Security Agency) Prism surveillance program created a major political shock.

7.4.3. *Job insecurity*

New technologies have enabled the creation of many highly skilled and often well-paid jobs, as well as new forms of work. The self-employed working for applications such as Uber (transport car with driver), or the delivery of ready meals (Deliveroo, etc.), generally have no employment contract, are paid on a "pay-as-you-go" basis, are pushed to work faster and faster (with the associated risks) and are totally subject to the conditions imposed by a company without having a "boss". These new forms of precarious work are referred to as employment uberization.

Seen even more is the precariousness of "micro-workers" who take on low-skilled activities offered on online platforms, for a generally very low pay per task. Behind the automatons are millions of "click captives", paid in some cases at less than one cent per click for tasks such as image identification, transcription and annotation, content moderation, data collection and processing, audio and video transcription, and so on. They are disposable, non-contract workers.

7.4.4. *The power of the big Internet firms*

A certain disenchantment corresponds to what has become of an Internet taken in hand by large groups tending to become monopolistic. Today, the market is dominated by a few giants who enact their laws, who behave like super-states with totalitarian temptations. Now, it is these groups that guide the development of institutions and society. Even more, it is their technology itself that shapes our world. In 2018, Facebook's turnover was over 55 billion dollars, while 117 countries in the same year had a GDP below that amount (source: World Bank). Its profit was close to 7 billion dollars because the company has no societal commitments (schools, a country's infrastructure, police, etc.), pays practically no taxes and its shareholders always ask for more dividends.

Are we moving towards the disappearance of nation-states or, at the very least, towards states without powers, towards an overthrow of politics and nation-states by companies with unlimited greed? At the end of 2019, Facebook intended to create a supranational currency, the libra; will it succeed? Will tomorrow's cyberdemocracy be subject to a few web giants or to a system driven by cameras and surveillance of personal data? Or is there a possible third path for a peaceful cyberdemocracy, where digital technology would be used for consensus-building rather than fragmentation, division and profit?

7.5. The digital divide

7.5.1. *From division to exclusion*

Being part of digital society is not limited to having equipment (computer, smartphone) or using social networks. The European Commission unveiled its 2019 ranking of the Digital Economy and Society Index for the 28 EU countries. France ranked 15th, far behind the best performing countries (Finland, Sweden, the Netherlands). The criteria were connectivity, human capital, use of Internet services, integration of digital technology and digital public services.

According to *France Stratégie* (a French research and forecasting, public policy assessment and proposal evaluation agency, reporting to the Prime Minister), nearly 14 million people are excluded or have difficulty with the use of digital technology[2]. Why these usage divides?

The first reason that comes to mind is the lack of access to the Internet; we talk about "white zones". At the beginning of 2019, the consumer association *Que Choisir* estimated that 6.8 million people were "deprived of minimal quality Internet access". These being rural and urban residents of less than 10,000 inhabitants. The situation is, however, tending to improve.

The second reason is age. Older people often don't have a computer or even a smartphone, and when they do have such equipment, they have real difficulties using it because they find themselves in a foreign world. Completing a tax return online is impossible without help.

---

2 https://www.strategie.gouv.fr/publications/benefices-dune-meilleure-autonomie-numerique.

The third reason is a lack of knowledge of digital technologies. Young people (almost) all have smartphones. Although they are assiduous users of the Internet, young people are mainly limited to using a few social networks and loading music or videos. Looking for a job, writing a CV and a cover letter (word processing) to send to a potential employer require more knowledge. Training in school curricula is probably very insufficient.

We have just been talking about the digital divide in France. What about developing countries? While mobile Internet is progressing rapidly on the African continent, data shows that three quarters of the population remain offline.

7.5.2. *Digital technology and education*

Education is a key factor in bridging the digital divide for both young and old. It is not a question of ensuring that everyone becomes a computer scientist, but that everyone can use the tools that are almost indispensable in today's society, while being aware of the limits and dangers of these tools.

7.5.2.1. *The school*

A Digital School Plan (*Plan numérique*) was announced by the French government in 2015: "Digital technology is not just a tool, it's not just pedagogy, it's not just content. It's also a culture, which means that every school pupil must be equipped with the means to understand what is read, what can be seen on digital tablets or computers, to understand the issues in terms of citizens-natured people, to also have a good analysis of what programming is, how a certain amount of content and resources are created…".

An ambitious goal! There are, in our opinion, at least three levels. The first level is the use of tools (tablets, for example) in the study of other subjects (French, geography, etc.): mastering access to information, knowing how to sort and choose it, detecting pitfalls. The second level is to allow children to have some distance from these tools and their misuse (harassment, etc.). All this must be part of the common building block. The third level is more centered on basic notions of computer science such as algorithms that develop logical thinking, coding, etc. (not everyone becomes a mathematician but everyone must know some mathematical basics). This can be part of school activities, with teachers trained for this. The use of sites such as code.org can be helpful to the teachers and even directly to the children. What is the status of the implementation of this digital plan?

7.5.2.2. *The training of adults and minorities away from these technologies*

Computer technology scares many adults, especially the elderly. Their training is done, for the most part, by associations and we consider that they must be helped, for example, by local authorities, because many citizens need it to be included in today's and tomorrow's society. The National Plan for an Inclusive Digital Society, launched in 2018 by the French government, is undoubtedly a step in the right direction.

7.6. Mastering the use of artificial intelligence

We have already pointed out the risks involved in certain uses of technologies based on algorithms associated with artificial intelligence. When mastered, AI is a tremendous opportunity. Altered, it could represent a great danger. Researchers, politicians and organizations such as the European Economic and Social Committee have highlighted some of these dangers.

In January 2019, the *MIT Technology Review* magazine published an article summarizing the six main risks of AI: autonomous cars (major technological flaws), political manipulation, killer algorithms (use of AI for military purposes, such as killer drones), facial recognition (electronic mass surveillance), fake news (threats to a healthy democratic debate) and algorithmic discrimination (algorithms trained from unequal data reproducing the stereotypes and discriminations of our societies).

AI is also an economic issue, and Europe is lagging behind the United States and Asia. In 2018, the European Commission announced a plan to inject 20 billion euros into AI projects by 2021 by Member States and the private sector. In 2019, it began work on the ethical aspect, with the presentation of its guidelines on the subject, based on the report submitted by a group of independent experts (researchers, philosophers, businesses, consumers, etc.). Seven main rules are put forward: AI systems must remain under human control and supervision, respect the main rules on personal data, rely on highly secure algorithms, be transparent, be traceable and ensure that they are accessible to the greatest number of people and not discriminatory. Wishful thinking or a prelude to legislation?

There is an absolute need for ethical reflection and legislation to control, if possible, the development of the use of AI.

7.7. The intelligent prosthesis and the bionic man

The very rapid progress made in the biological sciences, in nanotechnology and in computer science, especially in artificial intelligence, leads some to imagine a "new human" who would not be limited in physical or intellectual capacities, promising the abolition of old age, disease and death. This is still science fiction, but the "immortal human" is becoming a contemporary myth.

The first prostheses date back to prehistoric times, when humans began to stand on their own two feet because once they stood, they were only looking for one thing: to remain standing. Of course, prosthetics have evolved over time, especially as a result of the great wars that left many people disabled. The term prosthesis refers to an internal or external device that replaces or reinforces either a limb or part of a limb or an organ of the body to replace the compromised function(s). Our glasses, for example, are prostheses. The technical problems are different if they are substitutes placed outside the body or if they are implanted artificial organs. These two categories have made enormous progress, due to the introduction of new materials, advances in electronics, computer technology and, above all, a better understanding of how the human body works.

In just a few years, mechanical prostheses have rapidly evolved, and their performance has become increasingly impressive. Artificial organs are gradually emerging as a possible alternative to transplants. We speak of bionic prostheses, bionics being the science that aims to improve technology (especially electronics and computer science) by taking advantage of the study of certain biological processes observed in living beings. The bionic arm reuses nerves that were no longer solicited after amputation, and sensors will then interpret the nerve impulse triggered by thought to trigger the movements of the motorized prosthesis. The on-board electronics allow the artificial knees to restore walking as well as possible by analyzing both the environment and the movement of the contralateral limb to lock onto it.

Exoskeletons give paraplegics the ability to stand up or climb stairs. Using the signals emitted by the brain to regain the use of a limb is no longer science fiction.

Today's hearing aids can suppress background noise, but they amplify all voices indiscriminately. In new devices under development, the system receives a single audio channel with crossover sounds and then distinguishes between the different voices in this hubbub using artificial intelligence algorithms to amplify the sound of the conversation that most interests the listener.

The artificial heart will soon be a well-controlled prosthesis, even if its cost is very high (more than 100,000 euros). It works like a motorized pump, thanks to software and a state-of-the-art electronic system (microprocessor and seven sensors in particular), capable of analyzing the pressures at the entrance and exit of the ventricle after each beat, and adapting the cardiac output.

There is still the brain: brain chips are capable of monitoring and controlling various functions of the human body, but brain transplantation is not really considered, as a functioning brain; that is, a living brain would be needed as a replacement. So does a prosthesis make sense?

Today, prostheses are intended to repair a damaged or destroyed limb. But some consider that prostheses could improve the performance of a limb, and that some humans could use prostheses to improve the physical or mental characteristics of a human for this purpose. We arrive at the notion of the bionic man, a new echelon of the human species which would be reserved, of course, for one or more privileged classes. It is the shift **from repaired man to augmented man**, programmed to become completely artificial, advocated by Ray Kurzweil, the champion of transhumanism.

7.8. Transhumanism

If we can replace any defective part of the human body, if we can cure neurological diseases (if we cannot use a prosthesis), what becomes of the human being? Can we envisage an increase in our life expectancy or even our immortality?

Genetic engineering, which makes it possible to modify the genetic constitution of an organism, prostheses that can amplify our physical capacities, cognitive sciences, nanotechnologies, robotics and artificial intelligence: all the progress made (and that remains to be made) in these fields leads some to consider that the forms of humanity that we know are in the process of being outdated and that the posthuman; that is, what comes after the human, as well as the transhuman, is on the horizon.

This theory meets with many detractors, particularly among scientists[3] who consider that it is a childish ideology, a fantasy, with a risk of eugenics (prior selection of the best individuals to access transhuman technologies), that the body is not a machine, that aging is inevitable even if it takes place in better health, not forgetting that while life expectancy is 83.7 years in Japan, it is less than 60 years in a large part of the world (source: WHO). This theory also has a strong economic dimension, and the digital giants are interested in it at the risk of deepening social inequalities, because the cost of the individual's transformations is considerable (who could "buy" eternity or power?).

This debate on transhumanism has at least one merit: it pushes us to think about the future we want and the place we give to technology in our lives.

7.9. What kind of society for tomorrow?

A few personal reflections to end this book: I suggest you read the books by economist Daniel Cohen (2018) and historian Yuvan Noah Harari (2019), which provide an incomparably richer vision.

Digital technologies have made extraordinary progress in recent years and are gradually invading the world. At the same time, our world is plagued by sometimes violent conflicts, the questioning of the democratic ideal, development gaps that are difficult to bear, antagonisms about climate change and its consequences, etc. Does IT provide solutions? My answer is "no". I'll give an example. Mathematical models and supercomputers are making increasingly accurate predictions about the evolution of the ozone

---

3 Read, for example, the book by Danièle Tritsch and Jean Mariani *Ça va pas la tête: cerveau, immortalité et intelligence artificielle, l'imposture du transhumanisme* (Tritsch and Mariani 2018).

layer, pollution and climate. These technological advances have little or no effect on the decisions taken by the leaders of our planet.

In this chapter, I have presented some questions that our digital society must ask itself. Technologies alone will not solve the challenges of our world, but they can contribute to them.

The human species is creative and always in search of new ideas and technologies. The technologies associated with the digital world are neither good nor bad; it is up to our societies to use them so that they are at our service, and not the other way around.

An important question arises: Will we be part of these choices, or will they be imposed on us?

Bibliography

Abellard, A. (2018). Dans la tête des robots. *Le Monde*, 60, Special edition.

Berners-Lee, T. (2000). *Weaving the Web: The Original Design and Ultimate Destiny of the World Wide Web*. Harper Business, New York.

Berry, G. (2017). *L'hyperpuissance de l'informatique*. Odile Jacob, Paris.

Bouzeghoub, M. and Mosseri, R. (2017). *Les Big Data à découvert*. CNRS Éditions, Paris.

Bryant Randal, E. and O'Hallaron David, R. (2015). *Computer Systems: A Programmer's Perspective*, 3rd edition. Pearson.

Cohen, D. (2018). *Il faut dire que les temps ont changé*. Albin Michel, Paris.

Comer, D. (2018). *The Internet Book: Everything You Need to Know About Computer Networking and How the Internet Works*. CRC Press, Boca Raton.

Cormen, T.H., Eiserson, C.E., Rivest, R.L., and Stein, C. (2009). *Introduction to Algorithms*. MIT Press, Cambridge, MA, USA.

Davis, A. (2018). The WIRED guide to self-driving cars [Online]. Available: https://www.wired.com/story/guide-self-driving-cars/.

Delacroix, J. and Cazes, A. (2018). *Architecture des machines et des systèmes informatiques*, 6th edition. Dunod, Paris.

Harari, Y.N. (2018). *21 Lessons for the 21st Century*. Jonathan Cape/libri.

Hennessy, J.L. and Patterson, D.A. (2017). *Computer Architecture: A Quantitative Approach*. Morgan Kaufmann Publishers, Burlington, MA, USA.

INRIA (2018). Véhicules autonomes et connectés. Livre blanc no. 2 [Online]. Available: https://www.inria.fr/sites/default/files/2019-10/inrialivre-blancvac-180 529073843.pdf.

Julia, L. (2019). *L'intelligence artificielle n'existe pas*. Éditions First, Paris.

Kelleher, J.D. and Tierney, B. (2018). *Data Science*. The MIT Press Essential Knowledge Series.

Le Cun, Y. (2019). *Quand la machine apprend*. Odile Jacob, Paris.

Leroy, X. (2009). Formal verification of a realistic compiler. *Communications of the ACM*, 52(7), 107–115.

Newman, M. (2018). *Networks: An Introduction*. Oxford University Press.

Pujolle, G. (2018). *Les réseaux: l'ère des réseaux cloud et de la 5G*, 9th edition. Eyrolles, Paris.

Tanenbaum, A.S. and Van Steel, M. (2007). *Distributed Systems: Principles and Paradigms*. Prentice Hall, Upper Saddle River.

Tritsch, D. and Mariani, J. (2018). *Ça va pas la tête : cerveau, immortalité et intelligence articielle, l'imposture du transhumanisme*. Belin, Paris.

Index

Other titles from

in

Computer Engineering

2020

LAURENT Anne, LAURENT Dominique, MADERA Cédrine
Data Lakes
(Databases and Big Data Set – Volume 2)

OULHADJ Hamouche, DAACHI Boubaker, MENASRI Riad
Metaheuristics for Robotics
(Optimization Heuristics Set – Volume 2)

SADIQUI Ali
Computer Network Security

VENTRE Daniel
Artificial Intelligence, Cybersecurity and Cyber Defense

2019

BESBES Walid, DHOUIB Diala, WASSAN Niaz, MARREKCHI Emna
Solving Transport Problems: Towards Green Logistics

CLERC Maurice
Iterative Optimizers: Difficulty Measures and Benchmarks

GHLALA Riadh
Analytic SQL in SQL Server 2014/2016

TOUNSI Wiem
Cyber-Vigilance and Digital Trust: Cyber Security in the Era of Cloud Computing and IoT

2018

ANDRO Mathieu
Digital Libraries and Crowdsourcing
(Digital Tools and Uses Set – Volume 5)

ARNALDI Bruno, GUITTON Pascal, MOREAU Guillaume
Virtual Reality and Augmented Reality: Myths and Realities

BERTHIER Thierry, TEBOUL Bruno
From Digital Traces to Algorithmic Projections

CARDON Alain
Beyond Artificial Intelligence: From Human Consciousness to Artificial Consciousness

HOMAYOUNI S. Mahdi, FONTES Dalila B.M.M.
Metaheuristics for Maritime Operations
(Optimization Heuristics Set – Volume 1)

JEANSOULIN Robert
JavaScript and Open Data

PIVERT Olivier
NoSQL Data Models: Trends and Challenges
(Databases and Big Data Set – Volume 1)

SEDKAOUI Soraya
Data Analytics and Big Data

SALEH Imad, AMMI Mehdi, SZONIECKY Samuel
Challenges of the Internet of Things: Technology, Use, Ethics
(Digital Tools and Uses Set – Volume 7)

SZONIECKY Samuel
Ecosystems Knowledge: Modeling and Analysis Method for Information and Communication
(Digital Tools and Uses Set – Volume 6)

2017

BENMAMMAR Badr
Concurrent, Real-Time and Distributed Programming in Java

HÉLIODORE Frédéric, NAKIB Amir, ISMAIL Boussaad, OUCHRAA Salma, SCHMITT Laurent
Metaheuristics for Intelligent Electrical Networks
(Metaheuristics Set – Volume 10)

MA Haiping, SIMON Dan
Evolutionary Computation with Biogeography-based Optimization
(Metaheuristics Set – Volume 8)

PÉTROWSKI Alain, BEN-HAMIDA Sana
Evolutionary Algorithms
(Metaheuristics Set – Volume 9)

PAI G A Vijayalakshmi
Metaheuristics for Portfolio Optimization
(Metaheuristics Set – Volume 11)

2016

BLUM Christian, FESTA Paola
Metaheuristics for String Problems in Bio-informatics
(Metaheuristics Set – Volume 6)

DEROUSSI Laurent
Metaheuristics for Logistics
(Metaheuristics Set – Volume 4)

DHAENENS Clarisse and JOURDAN Laetitia
Metaheuristics for Big Data
(Metaheuristics Set – Volume 5)

LABADIE Nacima, PRINS Christian, PRODHON Caroline
Metaheuristics for Vehicle Routing Problems
(Metaheuristics Set – Volume 3)

LEROY Laure
Eyestrain Reduction in Stereoscopy

LUTTON Evelyne, PERROT Nathalie, TONDA Albert
Evolutionary Algorithms for Food Science and Technology
(Metaheuristics Set – Volume 7)

MAGOULÈS Frédéric, ZHAO Hai-Xiang
Data Mining and Machine Learning in Building Energy Analysis

RIGO Michel
Advanced Graph Theory and Combinatorics

2015

BARBIER Franck, RECOUSSINE Jean-Luc
COBOL Software Modernization: From Principles to Implementation with the BLU AGE® Method

CHEN Ken
Performance Evaluation by Simulation and Analysis with Applications to Computer Networks

CLERC Maurice
*Guided Randomness in Optimization
(Metaheuristics Set – Volume 1)*

DURAND Nicolas, GIANAZZA David, GOTTELAND Jean-Baptiste, ALLIOT Jean-Marc
*Metaheuristics for Air Traffic Management
(Metaheuristics Set – Volume 2)*

MAGOULÈS Frédéric, ROUX François-Xavier, HOUZEAUX Guillaume
Parallel Scientific Computing

MUNEESAWANG Paisarn, YAMMEN Suchart
Visual Inspection Technology in the Hard Disk Drive Industry

2014

BOULANGER Jean-Louis
Formal Methods Applied to Industrial Complex Systems

BOULANGER Jean-Louis
Formal Methods Applied to Complex Systems:Implementation of the B Method

GARDI Frédéric, BENOIST Thierry, DARLAY Julien, ESTELLON Bertrand, MEGEL Romain
Mathematical Programming Solver based on Local Search

KRICHEN Saoussen, CHAOUACHI Jouhaina
Graph-related Optimization and Decision Support Systems

DELAHAYE Daniel, PUECHMOREL Stéphane
Modeling and Optimization of Air Traffic

FRANCOPOULO Gil
LMF — Lexical Markup Framework

GHÉDIRA Khaled
Constraint Satisfaction Problems

ROCHANGE Christine, UHRIG Sascha, SAINRAT Pascal
Time-Predictable Architectures

WAHBI Mohamed
Algorithms and Ordering Heuristics for Distributed Constraint Satisfaction Problems

ZELM Martin *et al.*
Enterprise Interoperability

2012

ARBOLEDA Hugo, ROYER Jean-Claude
Model-Driven and Software Product Line Engineering

BLANCHET Gérard, DUPOUY Bertrand
Computer Architecture

BOULANGER Jean-Louis
Industrial Use of Formal Methods: Formal Verification

BOULANGER Jean-Louis
Formal Method: Industrial Use from Model to the Code

CALVARY Gaëlle, DELOT Thierry, SÈDES Florence, TIGLI Jean-Yves
Computer Science and Ambient Intelligence

MAHOUT Vincent
Assembly Language Programming: ARM Cortex-M3 2.0: Organization, Innovation and Territory

MARLET Renaud
Program Specialization

SOTO Maria, SEVAUX Marc, ROSSI André, LAURENT Johann
Memory Allocation Problems in Embedded Systems: Optimization Methods

2011

BICHOT Charles-Edmond, SIARRY Patrick
Graph Partitioning

BOULANGER Jean-Louis
Static Analysis of Software: The Abstract Interpretation

CAFERRA Ricardo
Logic for Computer Science and Artificial Intelligence

HOMES Bernard
Fundamentals of Software Testing

KORDON Fabrice, HADDAD Serge, PAUTET Laurent, PETRUCCI Laure
Distributed Systems: Design and Algorithms

KORDON Fabrice, HADDAD Serge, PAUTET Laurent, PETRUCCI Laure
Models and Analysis in Distributed Systems

LORCA Xavier
Tree-based Graph Partitioning Constraint

TRUCHET Charlotte, ASSAYAG Gerard
Constraint Programming in Music

VICAT-BLANC PRIMET Pascale *et al.*
Computing Networks: From Cluster to Cloud Computing

2010

AUDIBERT Pierre
Mathematics for Informatics and Computer Science

BABAU Jean-Philippe *et al.*
Model Driven Engineering for Distributed Real-Time Embedded Systems

BOULANGER Jean-Louis
Safety of Computer Architectures

MONMARCHE Nicolas *et al.*
Artificial Ants

PANETTO Hervé, BOUDJLIDA Nacer
Interoperability for Enterprise Software and Applications 2010

SIGAUD Olivier *et al.*
Markov Decision Processes in Artificial Intelligence

SOLNON Christine
Ant Colony Optimization and Constraint Programming

AUBRUN Christophe, SIMON Daniel, SONG Ye-Qiong *et al.*
Co-design Approaches for Dependable Networked Control Systems

2009

FOURNIER Jean-Claude
Graph Theory and Applications

GUEDON Jeanpierre
The Mojette Transform / Theory and Applications

JARD Claude, ROUX Olivier
Communicating Embedded Systems / Software and Design

LECOUTRE Christophe
Constraint Networks / Targeting Simplicity for Techniques and Algorithms

2008

BANÂTRE Michel, MARRÓN Pedro José, OLLERO Hannibal, WOLITZ Adam
Cooperating Embedded Systems and Wireless Sensor Networks

MERZ Stephan, NAVET Nicolas
Modeling and Verification of Real-time Systems

PASCHOS Vangelis Th
Combinatorial Optimization and Theoretical Computer Science: Interfaces and Perspectives

WALDNER Jean-Baptiste
Nanocomputers and Swarm Intelligence

2007

BENHAMOU Frédéric, JUSSIEN Narendra, O'SULLIVAN Barry
Trends in Constraint Programming

JUSSIEN Narendra
A TO Z OF SUDOKU

2006

BABAU Jean-Philippe *et al.*
From MDD Concepts to Experiments and Illustrations – DRES 2006

HABRIAS Henri, FRAPPIER Marc
Software Specification Methods

MURAT Cecile, PASCHOS Vangelis Th
Probabilistic Combinatorial Optimization on Graphs

PANETTO Hervé, BOUDJLIDA Nacer
Interoperability for Enterprise Software and Applications 2006 / IFAC-IFIP I-ESA'2006

2005

GÉRARD Sébastien *et al.*
Model Driven Engineering for Distributed Real Time Embedded Systems

PANETTO Hervé
Interoperability of Enterprise Software and Applications 2005

Printed and bound by CPI Group (UK) Ltd, Croydon, CR0 4YY